THE ALFALFA GUY

By Adam Corres

A Compilation of Surreal and Satirical Comedy Sketches

The Alfalfa Guy

Monologue: The Letters of Khafui

The World Through An Ice Lens

St Dunstan's Island

Dubious Company

Gavin The Bulb

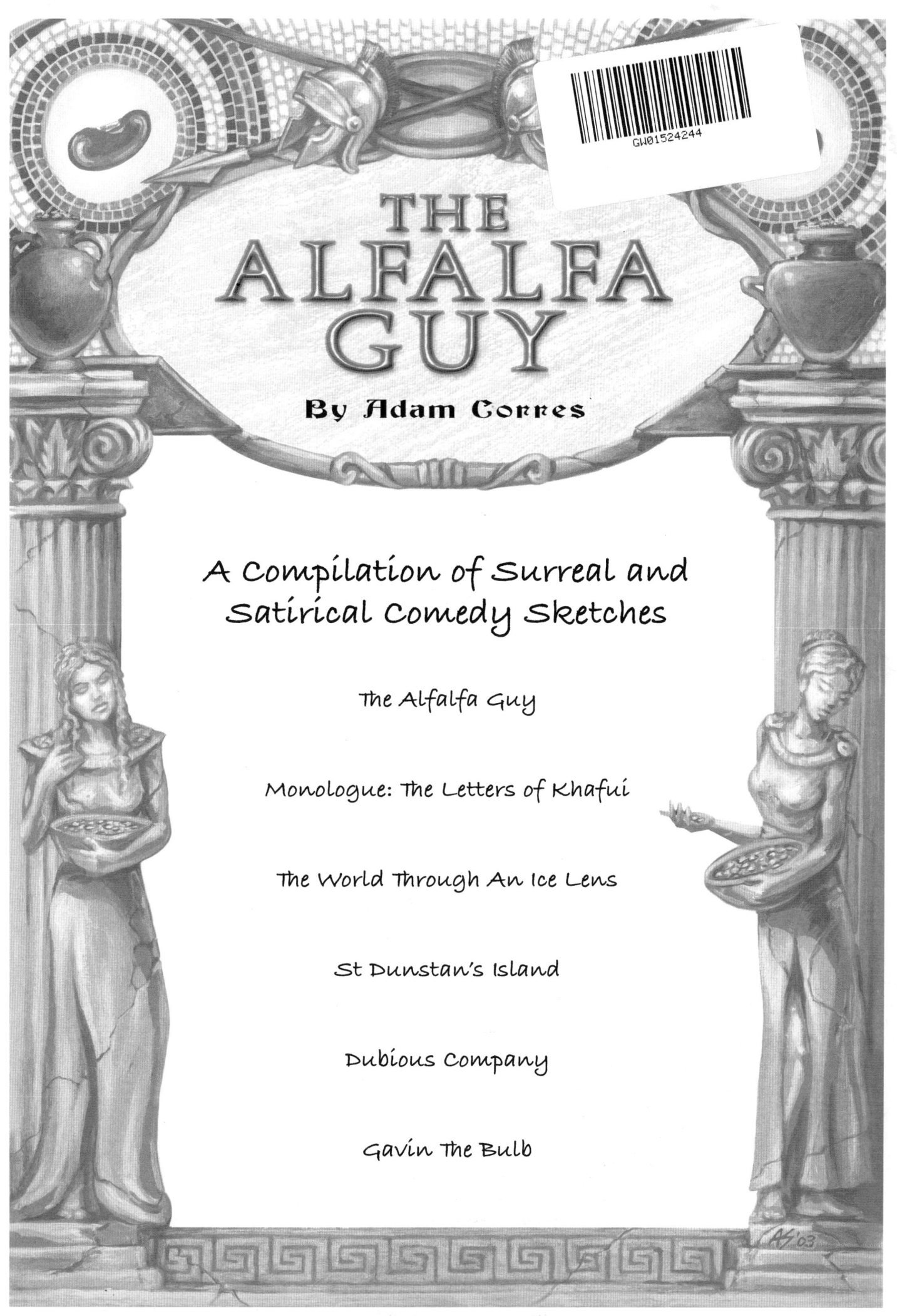

Copyright © 2003 Adam Corres

All rights reserved. Apart from any fair dealing for the purposes of research or private study, or criticism or review, as permitted under the Copyright, Designs and Patents Act 1988, this publication may only be reproduced, stored or transmitted, in any form or by any means, with the prior permission in writing of the publishers, or in the case of reprographic reproduction in accordance with the terms of licences issued by the Copyright Licensing Agency. Enquiries concerning reproduction outside those terms should be sent to the publishers.

The rights of Adam Corres to be identified as the author of this work have been asserted by him in accordance with the Copyright Designs and Patents Act, 1988.

Matador
12 Manor Walk, Coventry Road, Market Harborough, Leics LE16 9BP, UK
Tel: (+44) 1858 468828 / 469898   Email: books@troubador.co.uk   Web: www.troubador.co.uk/matador

First edition 2003

ISBN 1-904744-07-9

All characters in this book are fictitious, and any resemblance to actual persons, living or dead, is purely coincidental.

Typesetting: Troubador Publishing Ltd, Market Harborough, UK
Printed by Publish on Demand Ltd, London

Matador is an imprint of Troubador Publishing Ltd

INTRODUCING THE AUTHOR AND ARTISTS

ADAM CORRES

Adam Corres is a thirty-something who carries out unreliable duties at a major British university. Following a spectacularly de-railed career as a chef he now divides his time between agonising about the cricket, obsessive book collecting, occasional journalism for the Sunday papers, staring at bonfires and conserving endangered species of cacti. His first comic novel, *View from the Spoil Heap*, is scheduled for 2004. Adam has recently helped to found a group writing comedy scripts for television. His 'Ice Lens' sketch is currently being considered as a cartoon animation to be entitled *Bit Nippy Out*. An unrepresentative smattering of Adam's online work can be seen at http://www.DiverseBooks.com

ANNE STOKES
Illustrator of *The Alfalfa Guy*

Anne Stokes is already a legend in the world of science fiction and fantasy art. Her remarkable work appears on posters, rock band album covers, jewellery, clothing, computer games and magazines. Her licensed jewellery designs, known collectively as *Stokes's Stuff*, are familiar to convention goers everywhere, as is her greatly admired design for the annual *James White Award for Science Fiction*. Anne's website can be found at http://www.AnneStokes.com

DAVE HALLEWELL
Illustrator of *St Dunstan's Island* and *Gavin The Bulb*

David Hallewell is a popular cartoonist who happens to have a boring day job as well. He lives in deepest Lincolnshire with his wife, a rabbit and a flock of guinea pigs. His main interests are food, being asleep, films and real ale. The guinea pigs also share these interests. Despite years of excellent magazine work, this is the first time that David has illustrated in book form.

NEIL McCHRYSTAL
Illustrator of *Dragon Bashin'*

At the age of four, Neil got in a whole heap of trouble for drawing on the skirting boards. Since then he's graduated from crayons to acrylics; and from bedroom walls to the internet... via paper and stuff. Neil's work can be seen at http://www.Psychochicken.com

Dedicated to
Mary Boudon, who keeps me in wine

With further thanks to Paul M.V.C. for insidious criticism and lukewarm beer. Listen mate, your initials may be 75% PVC and add up to 1105 in Latin, but that won't get you a job in the real world.

THE ALFALFA GUY

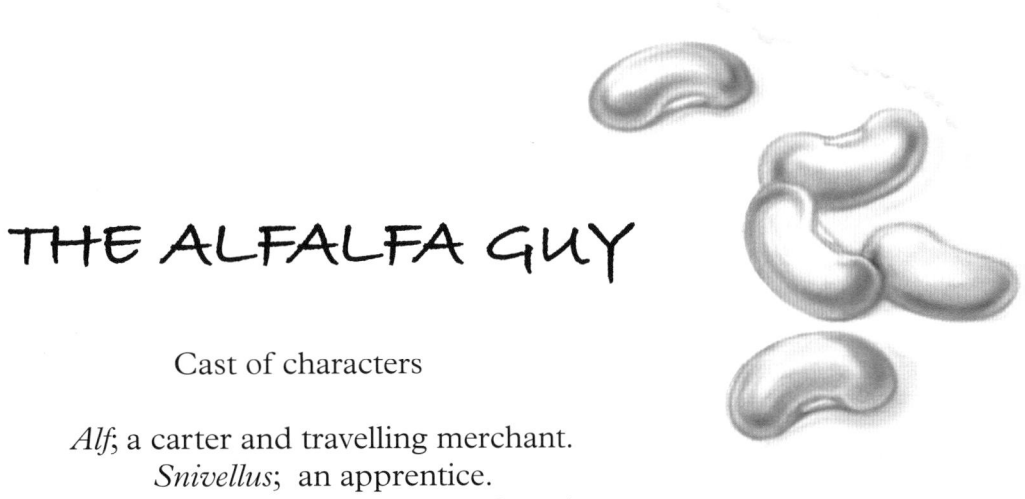

Cast of characters

Alf; a carter and travelling merchant.
Snivellus; an apprentice.
Centurion Bitpart; an Imperial Guard.

It could have been anywhere really. A plain, somewhere in the Roman Empire. A few miles from the town, one lazy late afternoon. Into view creaks a loaded cart and, gradually, voices can be heard…

Apprentice: "My brothers got 'prenticed to people with proper jobs. Not this draggin' beansprouts all over the place. Wassa point in that?"

Carter: "If you're going to be my apprentice lad, you'd better realise how important this here alfalfa is. Do you know what won the very first Roman victories?"

Apprentice: "Easy. 'Orses. Cavalry. I knew that, but now we don't use them much 'cept for passing messages. Foreign news, harvest is a bit iffy again, Granny's got her old trouble back on account of the weather. That sort of thing."

Carter: "Right. That's because our armies are full of conquered nations doing national service so they can become proper Romans. We wouldn't have those soldiers without the first battles, which we wouldn't have won without horses. What do Roman horses eat? Alfalfa. Ergo, the horse feed alfalfa is the only reason we've got a Roman Empire. We cart the alfalfa, ipso facto we've got the most important job in this here empire. Alfalfa's what made Rome great. We couldn't do without it. No horses and you've got the Athenians in Syracuse all over again."

Apprentice: "You're the best known Alfalfa carter, so that makes you the most important thing in the Empire, right boss?"

Carter: "That's right lad. I'm in charge. Now hop into the cart and try the seat of power. It's not just me of course. It's also the gods who smile down upon me. Deux ex Machina."

Apprentice: "What machine's that then?"

Carter: "The cart lad, the cart! Lose a wheel off that and we'd lose Germanica sure as sludge. Look kid, the Emperor may say otherwise, what with all his arches and his Trajic Column, but the difference between one country and another isn't much. We've got an advantage because everyone's working for us. We're disciplined and better equipped, but if you can't feed your horses it's the difference between all the triumphal arches you can tie a cart to and disaster! Silurians running the place. Or Greeks. They're the worst. Achilles sulkin' in his tent on account of doin' his tendon. Ajax up all night with some scrubber. In the end, the Greek army gave up on Troy and decided to try the next name on the atlas. It was a tough decade for Trowbridge."

Apprentice: "So we're better at being heroes than them then?"

Carter: "Your Greeks have different kinds of heroes, not just your officers see? They got this one bloke, Hercules, who got given the task of muckin' out some Assyrian bloke's paddock. Augean stables it was. Cleaning job. Except these horses had been eating really dodgy alfalfa for donkeys' years. Don't know where he got it. Off the back of a wagon I expect. Later on of course, the same bloke was making off with apples from the Hesperides."

Apprentice: "I used to go scrumpin'. So they make heroes out of ordinary people?"

Carter: "Yeah. Our lot wouldn't notice some snotty little dung-shoveller, but the Greeks set him amongst the stars!"

Apprentice: "I expect no one else wanted to do it. If I went to Greece, do you reckon I could be a star?"

Carter: "Who'd want to lad? When you look up at the night sky nowadays, there's more of them than ordinary people. We're the special ones, not them. The only difference is – they're brighter."

Apprentice: "So why do we bother with them Greeks?"

Carter: "You know all those statues they have stood around back in Rome? We import them all from Greece. They've got this girl called Medusa who can take one look and turn you into stone. Dreadful conversationalist of course, but she makes up for it on the creative front."

Apprentice: "Why are statues just of good looking people? S'not fair."

Carter: "Well, Medusa passes herself off as a portrait painter see? Advertises for models. Usually they're young athletes and sporty-types who need to make a few bob to keep their career going. When they drop in, she ducks behind the curtain and says "Strike a pose. I'll be with you in a jiffy. Just got to sort out my red ochre – it's only gone all fudgy again". Then she steps out, gives 'em the stare and turns them to solid stone. Makes a few obols flogging them off to tourists, which they then sell on the mainland for a bit of a mark-up."

Apprentice: "Why don't they get rid of this Medusa then? They should pull the whole temple down on top of her.

That would solve it. What's she gonna look like with a chimney on her head?"

Carter: "That's cutting off your own nose to spite your face, that is. If they got rid of Medusa, we'd have to chisel all the statues ourselves. It would take ages! We tried a public stone-carving competition once. Most of the entries were by the same Greek feller.

He had a thing about noses. The Senators didn't want the ugly things about the place, so we sold them off cheap to Easter Island and chucked in free delivery. Socrates, his name was, got banned from sculptin' and got told to go and do something else for a living. Of course, he was fairly philosophical about it. On the bright side, at least the stone athletes get to keep their looks. People gaze at them like rock stars. The Greeks do lose quite a lot of sports equipment that way, so at least we get to trade a few things back and everyone's happy. Haven't seen any statues arriving since we started supplying them with those shiny bronze shields though. Great burnish. See your face in them. Funny that."

Apprentice: "I heard about that Socrates in the market. They were selling scrolls for educating. At that price, you had to be part of the educated class to afford them, let alone know what you were reading. The Greeks sound like they've just about got it just right though. They've got a very fair way of looking at the world. Who's more civilised then? Us or Greece? Didn't Justinian invent justice?"

Carter: "There's more to it lad. The good thing about ethical philosophers is that we can feel superior knowing there's someone in our culture who thinks that way for a living. In the years to come, people will presume we all thought like that. Civilised. Enlightened. You see, the blokes the Emperor hires to string people up tend not to write epic poetry about it afterwards. They've seen enough to know there's always a chance it could apply to them. Except Caligula of course, but he was a bit odd. What with marrying that horse."

Apprentice: "What about Herodotus? He wrote about some very nasty stuff."

Carter: "He just wrote about people getting strung up in foreign places, so that's okay. Journalism. You can make up what you like. Can't see a future in it myself."

Apprentice: "That's eth-hicks is it? Do as I say and ignore what I did Thursday evenin'? Sounds like you can get away with anything in Greece. Why don't the gods tell 'em what's what?"

Carter: "They have different gods. A right mish-mash it is too. Our house-gods hang around the hearth and home. Vulcan stays put under Mount Vesuvius because it's the only logical place for him. Poseidon doesn't go having adventures all the time. They know their place. The Greek lot have strange ideas lad. Zeus is notorious for going to fancy dress parties as a shower. What a nutter. People like that need regulating. Don't think it impressed his date much as all the ordinary people had dressed up as gods for the evening. Always remember lad, if you're inviting a god to a fancy dress do, tell them it's a 'come as you are' party so they don't feel left out. It's different for Romans. You'd never get Italian gods mooching about dressed like normal folk."

Apprentice: "And bathroom appliances. Do you think that Aphrodite will ever visit Rome?"

Carter: "Nah. If she did, chances are the Emperor would seize her. Did you ever hear about that Greek bloke Archimedes? Thought not. There he was, stuck on his island being besieged by Rome and told to invent great siege engines. He didn't see the point of fighting, being more of a mover-'n'-shaker."

Apprentice: "Like us? If this cart don't move and shake I dunno what does. Weren't he a genius or somethin'?"

Carter: "That was the problem. He knew too much and had far, far too many side projects. He had some crazy idea about dried noodles in pots for long sea journeys. Then there were the tiny propellers for going on children's hats to keep their heads cool. He was always down the silver-smiths trying to get little strips of foil glued to his scratchcards. People wouldn't buy them without looking underneath, seeing as it was such a lottery. Scratch 'n' sniff never really took off either. Then there was that scandal when he was interfering with people's togas trying to attach washing instructions. Of course, circles were his main thing."

Apprentice: "Surely, they'd already been invented?"

Carter: "Yeah, but no-one wanted to dent his confidence by pointing it out. Particularly since he'd spent all that time studyin'. Credit where it's due though, I think he intended to bring a whole new dimension to circles."

Apprentice: "That's just balls if you ask me."

Carter: "Then there was something about the given value of pies. Epicurean mathematics that was. Philosophy and nibbles. He worked awful long hours and just ate snacks up in his room. Plates and cups everywhere. He invented Archimedes Screw to bring water in for washing up. Then there was that Archimedes Claw. It trundled along on a bar above the City Square. He lowered the claw, and picked up domestic staff who were loitering in the market place. Very useful for taking mucky plates out, they were. They didn't always bring them back though. One time the claw dropped down and grabbed his mother-in-law who was listening at the neighbour's fence. Very funny seeing her dangling above the rooftops with her bloomers showing. Of course the City Elders saw that and took it away for the war: Tippin' Roman ships up. Archimedes said that was as childish a use As picking up teddy bears in a box at the fairground, but no one was listening. Then he got caught keeping gold in his bath. The King soon pulled the plug on that one."

Apprentice: "If he was such a genius, how did Rome win then? Did we take his pencil away?"

Carter: "The Roman General Marcellus Detroitus was sent to attack him. Perfect choice, according to the philosophers. Marcellus used to be the kid who sat next to him class. When the Roman galleys arrived at the besieged Syracuse, the defenders could see all these great calculations and equations daubed on their sails. Someone called for Archimedes to interpret them. He interpreted them alright. Marcellus had written up all the maths that Archimedes had got wrong at school."

Apprentice: "That's not so bad really, even if it was in front of everyone."

Carter: "Only, that's not all. He'd added corrections!"

Apprentice: "That's evil."

Carter: "Yeah. Anyway, he lost his rag, which is never a good start to a bullfight. The gods immortalised the occasion. Even hundreds of years later, there's nothing so evil as double maths. It was worse in his day. You should have met Archimedes' Principal. Everyone said he had a hypnotising haircut."

Apprentice: "There must be more to being Greek than that. If it's just double maths and getting' turned to stone people'd live somewhere else. Somewhere quiet where they just do cookery."

Carter: "Violence. That's the only language they'll learn."

Apprentice: "Well, that and Greek."

Carter: "Funny lot though. Before Archimedes, the porcupine was the standard unit of measurement on Syracuse. You could say something was three porcupines long, a porcupine and a half high and two porcupines wide."

Apprentice: "They couldn't measure time with them though, could they?"

Carter: "Sure they could: One-porcupine-two-porcupine-three-porcupine-four-porcupine…"

Apprentice: "That's clever. How did they do multiplication?"

Carter: "Very carefully. Of course, porcupines don't come from Syracuse. They were part of the Roman export trade. Archimedes changed all that by explaining about numbers stored on paper, rather than spiky things which escape from their hutches and wander off down the high street looking for insects just when you want to do the measuring up for a new bathroom. That's why geniuses are so dangerous. Before him, if we'd explained about measuring things with sticks and theodolites, they'd just laugh and say they don't need to buy any 'cos sticks grow everywhere. We told them porcupines were unique, so they all wanted one. It's like telling people we've got Alfalfa X, with the miracle secret ingredient. Then again, our trading partners aren't quite as trusting as they used to be."

Apprentice: "How can they find out when there's nobody to ask? We could flog off a cartload of ex-alfalfa and a consignment of part used anteaters, then skip town before word gets about."

Carter: "Wouldn't work. The Greeks can tell the future, on account of Sybil, their Delphic Oracle."

Apprentice: "Whereabouts in Greece does she live then?"

Carter: "Thrace."

Apprentice: "My Gran could tell all sorts of mysterious stuff by looking into the stuck bits at the bottom of the cooking pot. She said she could see my future in beans. Of course, my sister wants to be a Goth."

Carter: "They're worse than the Celts for makeup. Problem is, tribes like the Goths and Silurians don't believe in Roman peace and civilised behaviour, so it's up to our lot to go over there and knock some Roman sense into them. Bang their heads together and burn their villages. In other words, civilise 'em, like us. Look lad, this is the thing to be. We're the difference in this world. We see the Empire and we make the victories. Veritas Vincit Victor Ludorum Alfalpheus!"

Apprentice: "This Victor bloke, what did he have against Silurians?"

Carter: "Oh, forget that. Just remember all the stuff we're here to protect. Hadrian had all them troops up north for years building that enormous well."

Apprentice: I thought it was wool, being sheep country."

Carter: "I expect it loses something in the translation. Impressive though. The Caledonians were probably feeling thirsty just looking at it. Goes on for miles it does, coast to coast."

Apprentice: "Why's it do that then boss?"

Carter: "State of the art Roman engineering lad. They're getting the water out sideways. Funny Spanish bloke, Hadrian. Too clever by half."

Apprentice: "Is he full of ideas? Like a cart full of beans with loose ones falling out the side?"

Carter: "Yep, except he's dead. It's Constantine or someone now, and do you know who put him where he is today? The bloke with the cartload of alfalfa! Me."

Apprentice: "Yeah! Er, and me."

Carter: "Well mainly me, since I've been doing it longer. It's the officers who take the credit lad. Stands to reason. You'd know that if you were an officer."

Apprentice: "Sarge, I'd like to go to Britannia some day. Do we deliver that far?"

Carter: "The Tin Islands? It doesn't do to go too far abroad. Wild anchovies wandering about popping out of the hedgerows and other strange stuff. One-eyed monsters. That's why they build the roads so straight, so they can hurtle down them scooping up the anchovies and still make it to market before the fish goes off. All the while keeping an eye out for monsters with their eye out."

Apprentice: "Anchovies come from the sea boss. It's common knowledge and I know it."

Carter: "You can prove what you like with facts lad. It's what people in public way-stations tell you they've seen with their own eyes and ears that counts. Experience, that is. None of your book learning. Only cost you a beer too."

Apprentice: "What will?"

Carter: "I'll tell you about it in the pub. Down here we only see anchovies in their winter habitat. In Britannia it's further north, so it's warmer 'cos they're closer to the sun. Stands to reason. That's why the Celts look so pasty white – they've been bleached. Do terrible things to you, the sun will. Just look at Daedalus."

Apprentice: "Weren't it Icarus, his son, who was the problem?"

Carter: "Exactly."

Apprentice: "Wassat place in the north? Wasn't Caledonia where the 9th Legion went missing? They marched in and were never seen again. Weren't they defeated?"

Carter: "Don't be silly. Your Picts and Scots aren't warlike people are they? I'll tell you what I think happened: There's your legion, marching past all the Scots…"

Apprentice: "In the baking heat…"

Carter: "…in the baking heat, with the sun glinting off their bear-skins, the great Eagle of the Ninth up front with all their shiny bits and pieces and things that say SPQR. A ruddy great flock of

eagles happen to be in the neighbourhood and see their eagle symbol. The Eagles say to themselves 'heigh-ho' – can't do the accent – 'eagle people!' and you know how birds take bright colourful things back to their nests? Well, I reckon there's a huge eagle nest somewhere on a high mountain peak full of little kidnapped legionnaires."

Apprentice: "What's in it for the ginormous eagle then?"

Carter: "I expect there's eggs the eagles want protecting from wanderin' dragons, and bits of fluff to keep in too. Baby-sitting jobs and things you can't imagine. Landing instructions. Either way it's going to be a pretty eyrie sight. On a clear day you can see for miles. Vertically."

Apprentice: "Why dunt they climb down?"

Carter: "It's probably an overhanging crag. They'd fall off and drop away forever and ever, or until they hit the ground. Whichever comes first. It's better to stay put. Of course, they'd have to adapt a bit to live at altitude. All their heavy kit would slide off down the mountain, so they'd have to improvise. Maybe use lighter stuff maybe bashed out of soup plates. Progress that is. The next generation of military equipment. It's cold up there, so they'd have to knit long woolly tights out of egret fluff. They'd have to do fashionable stripes or something so the baby eagles don't think they're worms. Socks are very important at altitude. When you get up there, it's survival of the thickest. Of course, Roman soldiers are the best in the world, so they'd teach them all that sort of stuff in basic training. You see, all perfectly logical. I'm surprised you didn't make the connection yourself. It must be really tough to be thick."

Apprentice: "Reckon so."

Carter: "The eagles probably don't understand why they haven't learnt to fly yet, but it's the Daedalus problem all over again: Too close to the sun. Maybe we should change our battle emblem to something eagles don't like."

Apprentice: "How about other eagles?"

Carter: "Nah. It's been done. Last time and the time before."

Apprentice: "What about elephants? Hannibal marched all them elephants right over the Alps!"

Carter: "Don't believe everything you hear lad. Elephants are mythical."

Apprentice: "I was over at that officers' mess a couple of evenings back."

Carter: "Delivering alfalfa."

Apprentice: "That's right, deliverin' alfalfa."

Carter: "Not eavesdropping."

Apprentice: "No. It was hard to hear everything through the tent flap, but them officers was sayin' we're taking over the world and it's all inevitable and to do with destiny! Of course Egypt's in denial."

Carter: "I think you'll find that's the other way round. Ooh! Me back's gone."

Apprentice: "You should try rubbin' some fish-sauce on that. That's what the bloke at the fish-sauce stall said when mine went."

Carter: "Shut up about fish-sauce will you? I thought you'd be sick of that after your 'experiment' in Sicily. They had to repaint the bath-house. The bloke with the amazing hat was livid. Did you do it on a bet?"

Apprentice: "Yeah. That merchant asked me where to unload. I said to myself "I bet he's daft enough to pour it where I say". I won a half denarius off myself. Spent it on a jar to carry fish-sauce in."

Carter: "I don't think we'll be welcome back. Talk about something else."

Apprentice: "Why do them legionnaires wear bear-skins?"

Carter: "Only some of them lad. It's so everyone knows how tough they are. In dispatches it says 'he had bare skin against the elements' and it shows up those wood loonies in Britannia a treat. 'Picti', they were called; 'painted people'. Silly idea really. Painting yourself blue to scare your enemies. Bunch of screaming turquoise jessies. How can you have a civilisation with them running around? I ask you."

Apprentice: "Well… them wood blokes are tougher aren't they? They ain't got nuffing on!"

Carter: "The difference is purely cosmetic I assure you."

Apprentice: "My Aunt Olive says Britannia goes on forever and ever and it's soddin' freezing."

Carter: "You haven't been there have you?"

Apprentice: "No."

Carter: "Right then. Well you heard wrong 'cos it's the cushiest posting in the Empire. Britannia's

where that bigwig Empress Helena comes from and she likes her creature comforts, believe me. Had to deliver her alfalfa once. Rush job for some party. Sixteen horses on her chariot just to go next door!"

Apprentice: "What about her litter?"

Carter: "Don't talk to me about litter! Next day it took a dozen slaves working around the clock just to clean it all up. Good party though. Annoying really. No one ever invites me to orgies."

Apprentice: "That's 'cos you've got a more important job boss! Deliverin' alfalfa and being the most important thing in the Empire!"

Carter: "That's right! So you mark my words 'cos that Britannia's a tropical paradise. The woad stuff is probably sun-block. Palm trees, figs, olives, enough fish-sauce to fill a Sicilian bath-house with. Again. Proper little officers' club. That's why that Boudicca wouldn't give it up. Even their place names sound delicate, mystical and somehow alluring. Ull, Grimethorpe, Aasleagh. No one's ever going to think our settlements are romantic. After all, 'Rome' is just the Etruscan for 'place where Romulus stopped to wash his smalls'."

Apprentice: "My Aunt Olive said that Syracuse was Sumerian for antler."

Carter: "It looks like your Aunt Olive is the major source of information in your family. Sounds like that General Coriolanus all over again. Pushed about by his mother and his lippy girlfriend until he runs away to war. Strange really, when you think about it, most people run in the other direction. Anyway after a year or two he comes back so covered in glory he can hardly see out and he's the Emperor's favourite sidekick. More useful than General Purposes, more listened to than General Directions and enough laurels to fill a hedge with. His nagging family were a different matter. The Emperor doesn't like busybodies. He lets the lions chase them round and round the Colosseum to teach them a lesson. Fair contest in my opinion. Cat-fight. You see, your lions and women are basically the same thing."

Apprentice: "Long nails, bad breath, laze around in the sun a lot?"

Carter: "Yeah. I mean, no. You'd have to see it to understand properly. That Emperor Nero was dead keen on circuses. He thought the people just wanted bread, music and circus entertainment to keep them happy. In the twelve years he was in charge, Rome didn't start a war with anyone. He was obviously mad, so we had to get rid of him. Then we had four civil wars in a year, so people relaxed what with everything being back to normal. It's complicated though. Seneca really ran the Roman republic."

Apprentice: "That's a lot of 'R's."

Carter: "No, it's true."

Apprentice: "What's the Colosseum for then?"

Carter: "You haven't been?"

Apprentice: "Nah."

Carter: "Right, well. Vespasian's big idea. They have chariot races with lions who whip at each other with their tails – it's very unpleasant. Then there's professional gladiators who pretend to hit each other with big wooden swords. It's a bit different from professional wrestling 'cos they can accidentally hurt each other every now and again, then the Emperor feels all queasy and sticks his thumb up."

Apprentice: "Up what?"

Carter: "Just up. It's not good when you incur the Emperor's wrath lad. You aren't allowed to be a gladiator any more and have to go below to help with the animals, never to see the light of day again."

Apprentice: "Does that happen a lot then?"

Carter: "By now there must be hundreds of ex-gladiators down there, helping with the animals. It's amazing the lions come out looking so upset. Unless of course they're jealous. The gladiators could be spending all their time pandering to that cuddly black and white bear."

Apprentice: "My Aunt Olive likes the Circus Maximus. She says that's where they do the chariots."

Carter: "Sometimes lad, sometimes I grant you. So what exactly does your Aunt Olive do?"

Apprentice: "She cuts and arranges flowers."

Carter: "What for?"

Apprentice: "To look nice."

Carter: "They already look nice. Is she compensating for something?

Your auntie won't know much about the exotic Celts of course. Very sensitive noses, the lot of them. Herodotus said they smelt bronze. The Brits feast on great banquets of Ship-Buttie, Frei-Urp and Newquay Broon. In Britannia you even get hares in your food. A very popular delicacy. They have great wisdom too. Their Druids have mastered the enchantment of magpies, the smartest of all birds."

Apprentice: "Do they do lots of spying for them and report back?"

Carter: "Yep, but the reporting back bit is where it all falls flat, 'cos the magpies only speak pigeon-English. The main problem conquering Britannia was the language barrier. In Latin we don't use the letter W. Caesar didn't know the time of day when the Iceni started disobeying the lav and referring to him as 'that oily vally'. A great empire we've got. No one's taking it seriously. Even the Spaniards are using our aqueducts as waterslides. Then there's that Stonehenge. They can't even tell us what it's for. Apparently, it was an ancient public project to celebrate the millennium."

Apprentice: "The millenum-mum of what?"

Carter: "They count things up in a different way lad. That's all changing now us Europeans are taking over, 'cos we're going to impose the Imperial system. Some things will stay the same though. Every Saturday evening they have games of kick-ball where you have to run along and boot the ball in a net. Woad against skins. Until we arrived, it used to be someone's head."

Apprentice: "They knocked someone's head off just to play a game?"

Carter: "Of course not. They're not Barbaric. They usually wait until one falls off naturally."

Apprentice: "It must be all that sunshine."

Carter: "It's embarrassingly easy to conquer a nation of kick-ballers. All you have to do is run near them and they fall over in agony. Pathetic. I can't see the sport ever taking off in Italy."

Apprentice: "Sounds wonderful. I wish I could join the army."

Carter: "No you don't lad. We conquered Britannia with just two legions, the VIIth & Xth. The rest of the army just ended up sat around in Aldershot peelin' turnips. That's not how to take in the Empire. At your age, what if I'd run off and been an Argonaut or something? I could have too. I even went for sporting trials for Herculaneum once. I would have made a great Argonaut, no two ways around, but they wouldn't have let me in. Discrimination, that's what I call it! Just because I weren't Greek."

Apprentice: "And it was hundreds of years before you were born. Er, and Jason & the Argonauts are mythical."

Carter: "Yeah, but apart from that… Look kid, your job's here, doing the shovelling and steering, thus freeing me up to concentrate."

Apprentice: "Why do I 'ave to do all the hard work?"

Carter: "Concentratin's the hard work laddie! How do you think a little squirt like Alexander took his empire from Macedonia to India? 'Evy lifting? I'm more your officer material, see. I'm cerebral; beloved of Cerberus."

Apprentice: "Even so, boss. It's good to travel."

Carter: "Very dangerous thing. You can get carried away travelling. Crossing the Alps f'rinstance, strange creatures all covered in hair can jump out in front of you in the high passes, waving their arms about and making strange inhuman noises! You have to run away, quick as you can. Then with all that snow, you don't know where you are and you have to make the best of it and live there. After a bit you grow all this long straggly hair to stay warm, and it gets everywhere. Even in your eyes, so you can't see out properly. After that your best chance is to find a mountain pass, wait for a traveller to come along and step out in front of him to ask directions. That might be a problem 'cos of all the hair that gets in your mouth, so you have to make do with mumbling and hand-gestures."

Apprentice: "I expect they'd be very helpful. What about joining the navy? That way you might even get to visit 'The Colonies'. You know, in the New World – Ireland."

Carter: "The navy's the most dangerous thing of all son. The world's flat, see? The water's constantly running away, pulling you towards the edge of the world. You can't sit down for a minute without getting dragged away. That's why all our galleys have those sticks out the side. It's to slow them down."

Apprentice: "Where's the best place to avoid then boss?"

Carter: "Fridgia used to be the coldest land of all, since it's over the edge of the world. Then they discovered Permia behind it, where it's so cold everything's gone blue. The woad blokes wouldn't stand a chance of spotting each other if they lived in Permia. In the time of Ragnor-Rok some whacking great dragon swallowed the sun. The dragon used to live in Caledonia, but I expect every time it went to take eggs from a huge eagle's nest all these little soldiers jumped out and started with the javelins and chucking stuff. The dragon went off to Permia after a week or two of this behaviour, as frankly, that's the frozen limit."

Apprentice: "My Aunt said Phrygia was in west-central Anatolia, part of the Persian Empire of the Middle East."

Carter: "This is a different Phrygia. They're twinned. The Fridgians use their sand for road-gritting."

Apprentice: "The high priests told our dad the sun was driven around in a chariot."

Carter: "That's our sun lad. They've got to use the spare, which doesn't have a chariot. That's how the dragon managed to catch up with it so fast. Probably gave the poor thing dreadful indigestion when it did. Don't go delivering to Permia. As soon as you see a dragon, it'll take you away and eat you soon as look at you. Take away flame-grilled Romani with spicy alfalfa side salad. Meals on wheels."

Apprentice: "How do you know everyone who's seen dragons got took away and eaten?"

Carter: "Obvious. No-one ever tells you they've seen a dragon, so it must be true."

Apprentice: "Doesn't anyone live in Permia now?"

Carter: "Yes. The Norse people live there. They invented the days of the week.

Apprentice: "What's that day with a turd in it?"

Carter: "Saturday. Thursday is the day named after Thor, their thunder god, Saturday's for Saturn and Monday is named after the great god Mun. He's the god of going back to work when you don't really feel like it."

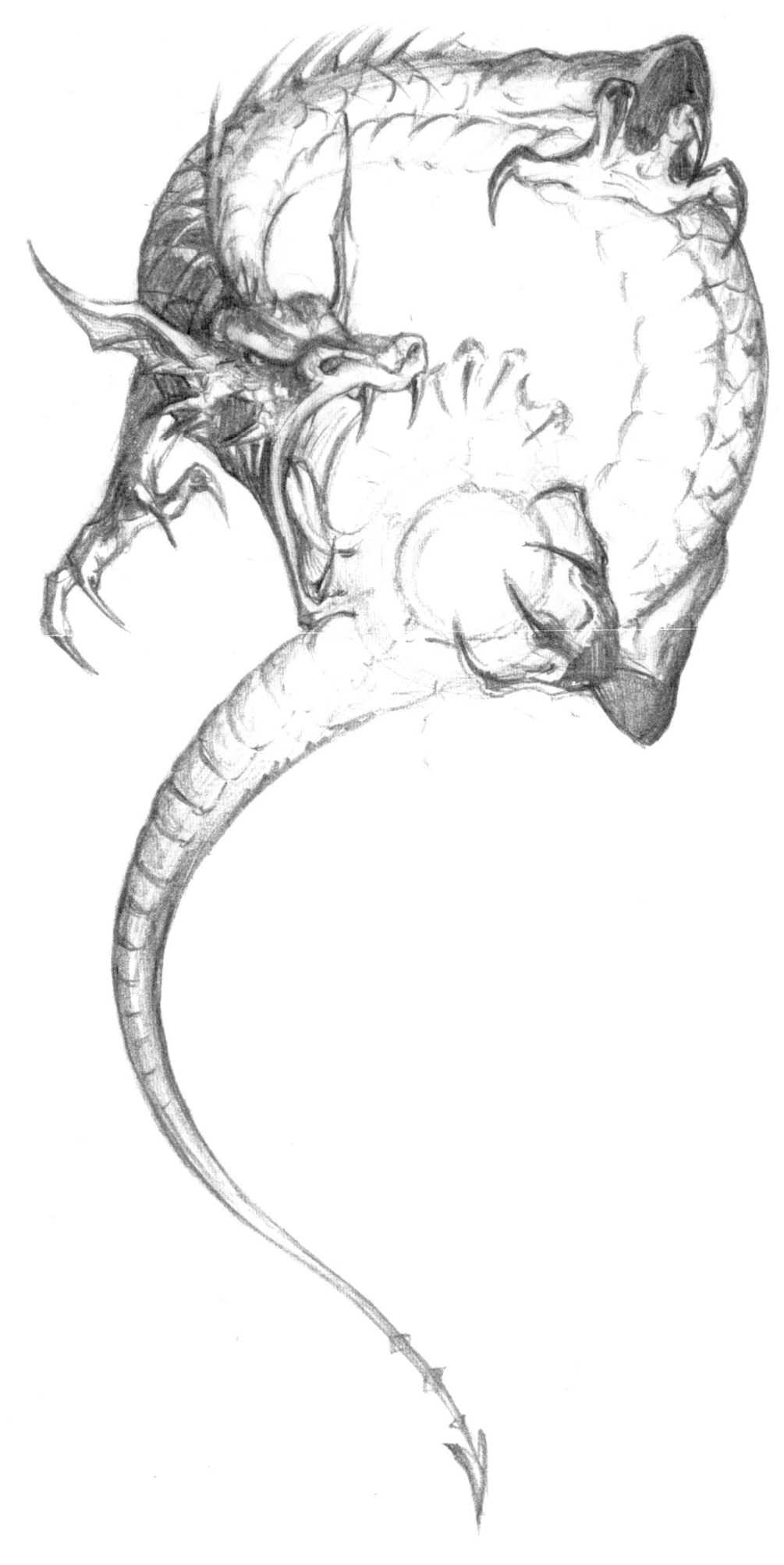

Apprentice: "Even Permia sounds more fun than this trudgin' about. I could um, h-emigrate."

Carter: "You should stick with the Empire lad. You might become somebody. Governor of the Tin Islands, maybe. What the all-knowing Tacitus called 'The land at the extremities of the earth'."

Apprentice: "Apart from Fridgia and Permia."

Carter: "Emperor Augustine got so important he named a month after himself – August. Of course, August is a flood month in Sogdania, which is why they don't like Romans very much. If you made it to the top of the pile, you could invent your own month too. 'Snivellus' would have to be one of the wet and dreary ones though. It's got that sort of sound. Short month. They'd probably slip it in between January and February and add lots of bank holidays so no-one complains."

Apprentice: "Wouldn't that upset the astrologers?"

Carter: "Any astrologers worth their salt would have written to complain before we thought of it. You stick to what you know. For ordinary people there's nothing that matters so much as a hill of beans."

Apprentice: "Someone else could take over. It's just a cartload of beansprouts after all."

Carter: "You'd never shift the stuff if it was just beans lad. Local commanders have fads. They won't just let their ostlers buy anything. Nowadays it's all about product enhancements. Additives. Alfalfa and olives for the Italians…"

Apprentice: "Not fish-sauce then?"

Carter: "No. Just vegetarian for the low countries, spicy for sellin' to the Persians and garlic & horse flavour for the horses in Gaul. Cook-in sauces too. Two for the price of one. We just make the price of one twice as much, see? Bargains. People will spend a fortune to save money. You have to be careful with the prices though, or Zeus flattens you with a thunderbolt. He gets uppity with overcharging."

Apprentice: "I had no idea sellin' beans was that complicated. It's a cut-throat world int-it?"

Carter: "You don't know the half of it. In business you've got to be clever. We could deliver beans in those special sacks which keep them warm and damp. They sprout like billy-o within a week or so and they have to be fed to the horses straight away before they go off. In a couple of weeks they're desperate for more feed and we show up just at the right time to sell them more. Then they thank us for it! 'Calculated obsolescence' they call that. It's to make you buy more. I hope it doesn't catch on. In the future you could have a brand new cart for three seasons, then it deliberately falls apart with rust just so you have to buy another one."

Apprentice: "They'd never get wood to rust boss, unless you're talking about something else. Rust is irony."

Carter: "Then there's your niche marketing. They even have little beetles in it for the Egyptian lot. Course, they don't get a choice. By the time you've got it to Egypt there's little beetles in everything. Strange place, Egypt. That Cleopatra more than makes up for it though."

Apprentice: "Is she as pretty as they say? Have you seen her then?"
Carter: "I saw her stelae once."

Apprentice: "It's amazin' the guards let you get that close."

Carter: "You have to watch your step over in Egypt. All the cons they've got going beggars belief."

Apprentice: "Beggars, was that?"

Carter: "Yes."

Apprentice: "Not…"

Carter: "No. They've got one where they made the whole population put up some enormous stone mountains and promised they could fit everyone inside and live for eternity with sharp razor blades."

Apprentice: "I suppose beards would be a problem, what with all those people together forever and ever."

Carter: "It was another trick. Just for the King, see? You can't trust them. Then there's all that pyramid selling. You can't have proper trade without confidence. Our trading is blessed by the gods. If you cheat, they strike you down. In Egypt it's all different. They aren't on the ball. Take Osiris, god of the underground for instance. The priests can hardly hear him he's so congested. Oh, never mind all that. Talk won't sell beansprouts. I was thinking. We should have a slogan like 'It's a bean, but where hasn't it been?'. We could paint it on the side of the cart."

Apprentice: "That'd make them hungry boss."

Carter: "Don't be daft lad. Horses can't read. On second thoughts, I'd be surprised if you can."

Apprentice: "What's the town after this one then?"

Carter: "Can't remember. They all look the same nowadays. All the same stalls in the forum no matter where you go, that sort of thing. Same head on the money. It's the only way they can understand it all. Empires are all about standardisation. 'Course, some people spell that with a z."

Apprentice: "We're almost there boss. Look at them Imperial Guard in their purple uniforms. The Emperor must be visiting. They'll want to search the cart. Cor! How do they do purple then? Is that officer material?"

Carter: "It's a natural die, lad. They raid the gaming pits once a month, take all the worn-out dice, crush 'em up, recite the invocation to Hecate, add a snail for good measure and Bing!"

Apprentice: "Bing!? That's silly. Have you really been to all them places just deliverin' alfalfa?"

Carter: "So you know better do you? Alfalfa shoveller third class Snivellus?"

Apprentice: "Sorry boss. I didn't mean to…"

Carter: "Make sure that you didn't. You can learn a lot from me, you can. This here empire wouldn't work without the likes of me."

Apprentice: "Yes, Boss."

Carter: "If you know your place, and do as you're told with the unloadin', on the way back I might tell you the story of the Minoans and the giant octopus. They had an empire too you know. Just like ours, only the Minoans were small fry."

[the cart rumbles up to the city gate]

Centurion Bitpart: "Take that 'orrible cart round the back. You aren't coming in here."

Apprentice: "Don't you be rude to him! He's in charge of the Roman Empire!"

Carter: "Shut up kid. Keep yer head down."

♛ THE LETTERS OF KHAFUI ♛

An Acknowledgement

Before releasing this correspondence into the community, I should first explain the noble origins without which it would not have been written. In 1931, Evelyn Waugh wrote the book 'Remote People' to catalogue his journalistic experience of touring Kenya, Tanganyika, British Aden, Uganda, Congo and ultimately Haile Selassie's Abyssinian empire. Unlike the Benin Empire, Selassie (Ras Tafari Makonnen) had based the model for his court on modern western cultural influences. In an Africa which did not quite understand what he wanted, the minor practical absurdities that the west has developed a comfortable blind spot for soon became blatant.

In October of 1932, Waugh wrote of an emperor called 'Seth' who struggled against reality and nature to impose a foreign culture on a decaying African backdrop. Seth was a thinly disguised Selassie (who was still very much alive), but the character soon evolved into something more intriguing. Instead of being a commentary *about* Africa, looking at the situation from this new perspective formed an insinuation of how the west had *treated* Africa.

Much has changed in the last seventy-five years. The Emperor was deposed, twice, Abyssinia 'Jewel of East Africa' is now troubled Ethiopia and the British have lost Aden. The Emperor is today regarded as a god by the Rastafarians of the West Indies. In a world forced to accept rapid globalisation, it might once more be a healthy time to review our cultural perspective. Although this new character is less subtle, and has a new period of international history to draw from, the mechanism remains the same. If it makes you feel uncomfortable, I wrote it for you.

P.S. Scientists agree that every year nine million tons of elephant crap falls on Africa.

Office of His Imperial Majesty
The Palace
Abu-Shantry
African Transcrabia

The United Nations Secretariat
Department of International Aid and Development
The High Street
Geneva
Switzerland

1st Wednesday of March.

Hello. May the season of the rains bring you prosperity. I am Khafui. I, Khafui, Fulcrum of the Seas, Emperor in Absolute of African Transcrabia (not Belgian Transcrabia, which is all on the mainland), The All Powerful, My Virility Inexhaustible, My Progeny Defies All Calculation, Aged 25, Bachelor of The Sciences of The Portsmouth Universities am writing.

I am writing this because of unfortunate upsets that are happening. This is not one of those letters the Nigerians are sending asking for money. We get those too. This is entirely other. I am rocking with chaos. My loyal subjects are leaving when I turn around and they have gone. This is at the wits end. Even the loyal ministers who are swearing to me and the man from the bank. All gone. Scarper down the docks. Only my loyal secretary is left. He is not typing this as he says he's not that kind of secretary. He is very stuck-up man, from Solihull. I think I trust him better if I am writing this as he says one thing and means other even though he's imported by special agency, with references too. Houseboy says secretaryman only still here as when he gone to the docks he find boat is already full with the loyal ministers doing runner. Houseboy is cheeky liar and not loyal at all. Houseboy's mother is very helpful at times. Sister is of little help and very dirty with the spitting on the rugs.

It is not good here. It is all gone hideous. There are the foreign powers wandering the seas and the plasterwork on the palace roof is falling off with the action of the vines and the little brown monkeys. I write to your Attenborough about them, but he does not write with money. He is of little help, same as houseboy sister. I will send pictures next time. I am making proclamation today and no one is listening! Cook is pretending to write down and then wander off when my back is turned and I see he is writing list about okra and yams. He is in for it when I catch with him. I will throw royal assegai at him with divine force come showing up time again at elevenses.

I am Khafui. I am great humanitarian. Next country over is having turbulence and civility war. Turbulence is a good word. It is meaning to make froth up like bananas and milk. I found this word in best medical dictionaries. The war froth from next door is called refugee. I am making offer to them to be the peoples of my country. We have less peoples now as they are going to the docks and not always coming back. I make proclamation and pin it to telegraph poles myself to make sure it is done as I proclaimed. Best pins. Made in Sheffield. I will collect back later. It says 'I am Khafui, da-de-dah etcetera, etcetera. Come and live in my country. Be of Peace and Free! No peace off on the mainland for you. We don't take slaves any more as that all long times ago. We have many jobs at the Palace and with best pay too for when Treasury Minister gets back from overseas investments in the name of the peoples.' He is very loyal man. He has many ties from your Austin Reeds. I am taking some of them on top occasions. If I am inspecting your country I will wear.

There are many top things in my country we can trade. We have the best of everything to swap for your help with developments. My supply is inexhaustible and I am speaking the best English now. Even some French, who are the powers wandering my seas. I see you have the French in Switzerland too. How do you stop them wandering your seas? They say they don't understand English, but they do when I make the Anglo-Saxon gestures. They are at sea a long time, then they come to discuss with houseboy's mother. The French tell Khafui not to let ships of the Americans stay as they put tin drink cans on the beach all night and their women speak with the voice of the electric saw. They are also allergic to nuts and it would be my fault. I looked for this in best medical dictionaries and I know it to be true.

I am writing long enough now and have put in postcards of my beautiful country and a few nuts for samples for your big scientist to test. They are the best and no need to test. The monkeys eat them and they are very active and pull tiles off the roof at night. They jump up and down and make the squeaks above houseboy's mother room. I think they don't like her much. They also eat insects under the tiles. Insects look different to nuts and no concern because we take them out now. Please to be sending your aid as tribute below. Also be sending your development. Do not send with anyone other than the French sailors because they say it is better that way and it won't be my fault. Urgently, these are the things:

Roof tiles, 184, 14×14inches, whatever colour you have there.
Much strong netting for the monkeys, with holes bigger than nuts (encl).
Hoops to regulate size of nuts to international standard.
Loyal servant to write things down especially morning doing of the proclamations.
Message to refugees in own language say don't run through our country to other countries.
New flags which are not tatty, see postcard top corner (ask your Austin Reed).
Honest Finance Minister with much trouble getting around. Not from agency. Maybe metal leg. You decide. What do you do?
Spikes for tin drinking cans, for when the Americans come.
Signed photo to me of your king so I can show loyal subjects my best new friends.
French dictionary. I must proclaim in French also or they claim don't understand.
Bicycle tyres, 28inch, for our industry.
Shirts (to go with the ties). Must have collars of medium size.
Send people home who are there, but should be here. They have no permissions.
Regional developments. You decide.
Submarine protections. I will grant you use some of my seas by return. To please stay on the surface and fly my flag (for safety reasons from my Imperial Navy, who have a confidential boat, which can not be recognised).
Other kind of secretary who can work typewriter. Agency is okay.
45rpm records and businesspeople for receptions.
Company that puts head on stamps.
Company that lends money against income for stamps.
Teacher to show public to write.
Dustbuster approved to international standard and batteries.
Addresses of people who are of help.

There is much I am to attend to and no one else today.

Yours in serenity,

H.I.M. Khafui I, Emperor in Absolute

Office of His Imperial Majesty
The Palace
Abu-Shantry
African Transcrabia

The United Nations Secretariat
Department of International Aid and Development
The High Street
Geneva
Switzerland

2nd Friday of September.

Hello. May the season of the sun dry up the beetles in your fields. It is Khafui here again. I, Khafui, Fulcrum of the Seas, Emperor in Absolute of African Transcrabia (not Belgian Transcrabia, which is all on the mainland), The All Powerful, With Virility Inexhaustible, Progeny Exceeding Calculation, Aged 26, Bachelor of The Sciences of The Portsmouth Universities am writing once again now.

Unfortunate upsets are happening less often. I am getting hang of it. Many boats are flying my flag today as it is convenient. Even some big ships which have never been to my country, they are so happy with what I have done. I have a new Regional Development Minister. She is called Greta and she is a project student on 'year out'. She has made application and we have been awarded very large financial grants to fund our rice farming industry. This is wonderful now. I did not even know we had rice farmers. It is a surprise and joyful because I was told rice can not grow without rivers and floodplains of which we have none. This is quick progress beyond all possible human expectation. The people will be most pleased.

It is the dry season. The cattle have mouths like letterboxes, as with British President's wife. Thanks you also for the netting. We have caught many monkeys and sold them to the restaurant in the docks, where the food is fast for travellers. It is very popular and they ask for more. Tell Attenborough not to come now. Also send less roof tiles next year. This is progress too. Royal lavatories are still backing up, but I have proclaimed the hospital in charge of this, so is all okay. They will draw out the dung and dry it in the season of the suns to use as fuel with all medical safety thought of against the epidemics. It is top recycling.

I need to ask about French. The dictionary is not helping. Houseboy's mother has taken more rooms at the Palace now. She sets up 'Informal High Commission' upstairs. French sailors wait outside to see houseboy's mother and discuss. She has many, many conference and is calling herself 'Madame' to please French visitors. I, Khafui, do not wish French Informal High Commission to be in the Palace, but the sailors say if I interfere it will be international incident and everything will be my fault. It is bad and the monkeys are much worse now with the jumping about at night and squeaking. Many girls from the village are coming each day to work at the High Commission in the processing of applicants. They dress in colourful things in the name of international relations. The police chief is volunteering personal security for them, which is very kind. He has a new foreign car, bringing further dignity to our country.

The houseboy is going to the boarding school in England. It is a long way and many girls wave him bye. I would travel with him to advise wisdom, but Royal finances have not yet returned from Treasury Minister's trip to find top investments abroad. He is very loyal and will be coming back soon. I have proclaimed this at the bank.

The little monkeys are most excitable today with the removal and digestion of proclamations. They are hooligans of limited help. Greta has proposals to print proclamations in the ink of the spiky stonefish, which carries much sickness. Greta says most disappointing and regrettable things of our national animal. There are worse things. She will get used to them.

There are to be less fish this year. French sailors say the people can't fish at the usual places from now because of the nuclear testings. They say I must proclaim this. I tell them we do not want this because it is not safe. The sailors say the reason it is not safe is because there has not been the proper testings. They say no testings and my people will be in great danger like in all the years before and it will all be my fault. They give me traditional drinks in friendship and say I am very wise. There will be other places to fish.

The waters are disturbed this year, despite the season of the sun. The are big ships with the cargo of wasteful toxics which can never be docked in the international ports. Many are resting in international waters near Abu-Shantry docks, which would not be tolerated by the Admiral Lord Nelson, also a graduate of The Portsmouth Universities. They say my map of the international waters is the wrong scale and is changed by treaty. I have written to Portugal for new maps as they are the very best of all explorers, with the trading of the slaves.

Your development instructions were most evident. All the powers agree I should have a 'free market economy'. I must give the market what it wants, then we can have the progress. To this end I have proclaimed Garth to be the Minister for Business. He is Greta's boyfriend and he is with a business diploma from Johannesburg, so is already the top man. Greta wanted him to be Minister for Customs and Docks as she calls this the most profitable ministry. She asks why it only breaks even every year and the Customs Chief is of legendary wealth, even known as far as Nigeria. She must stop these disloyal insinuations. He is my most reliable subject and is popular beyond the seas with his invitations. There is no reason to cheat as he is respected with top investments and the private resources. The loyalty is beyond question when he is here and all other ministers scarper down the docks quicktime. Garth will bring business. I have proclaimed and Greta has written this down.

I hope the rains will come early. There was witnessed one dark cloud over the Palace this month, to which the little brown monkeys shrieked and threw roof tiles. It soon burned away and the monkeys were no longer evident. As with the secretary man, who people say passed messages to Belgian Transcrabia and was a Bolshevik with the working to the rules.

In the next door country there is no fighting now, but there is no food. The international agencies give them many goats and are most helpful. The people can milk the goats and keep them for meat later. After the rainy season it turned bad. Goats ate all the crops in the fields and the people have no seedcorn for next year's plantings. The people have nothing to eat except the goats. The powers that are evident in the seas have lent them money, to pay back from next season's seedcorn, and more goats too. They are most generous and advanced.

I am Khafui. I am a great humanitarian, as befitting the Prince of the Chiefs of Sepu. It is wrong to lend money the poor peoples can't pay back. I will give the money to help with this debt when Finance Minister comes back with investment profits. Khafui will end this poverty and refugees. I will proclaim this soon. How will this be made fair? I have used my head. When I don't do this it all goes hideous. Greta has researched which place has the most 'per-capita' debt owing to all other countries on Earth. This is United States of America. I will send all spare rice money. Maybe goats too.

There is much I am to attend to and no one else today.

Yours in serenity,

H.I.M. Khafui I, Emperor in Absolute

Office of His Imperial Majesty
The Palace
Abu-Shantry
African Transcrabia

The United Nations Secretariat
Department of International Aid and Development
The High Street
Geneva
Switzerland

3rd Thursday of January.

Hello. May the season of the winds separate your chaff. It's me. We, Khafui, Fulcrum of the Seas, Emperor in Absolute of African Transcrabia (not Belgian Transcrabia, which is all on the mainland), The All Powerful, With Virility Inexhaustible, Whose Progeny Defies Calculation, Aged 26, Bachelor of The Sciences of The Portsmouth Universities am writing with messages of utmost necessity. It is also the age at which I must marry, so send explicitly your lists of suitable Empresses at child bearing age and notes on character and defects.

It is all gone hideous! Unfortunate upsets are everywhere. Houseboy's mother and sister have gone to live with houseboy in England and there have been no permissions. It is so quiet here now and the wild creatures are mostly behaved. I have been to inspect the rooms upstairs and I do not now think this was an Informal High Commission at all. I have found most unpleasant things. They are taken away altogether and buried in municipal grounds. The Palace drains are still blocked, but the responsible hospital says they are most busy with new diseases among the girls from the village. If the cholera happens now they will be for it.

The Minister for Business has taken immediate steps. It is to do with the commandeering of the zoo. The police chief has facilitated this with the pointed stick and shouting. He has explained much, but I am not to visit because of the snakes they are keeping there and the poisonous detriments to my Royal Person. I have seen the zoo before. There is one large pen and a colony of little brown monkeys who live inside it around one old monkey of a different shade who excavates a nose and displays much bottom. There are brown monkeys outside in great numbers, but they do not jump in because of the ferocious shrieking bottoms. Some children go to watch and learn about nature, but no money is made. The Business Minister has spoken to many zoos and has reported to me that the cage will now be used for the display of magnificent tigers. The people have been filled with excitement and directly wished to help, especially with the strengthening of the wire. I am most encouraged by their displays of loyalty and getting behindness which will continue under my top leadership.

It does not stop there. The Minister has arranged for contracts to be drawn with the best satellite television broadcasters. We have had experiences with television before, but it is to be different now. In my father's time there were radical communist elements who set up a broadcasting station and spent many months with television propaganda asking people to join rebellions and overthrow dynastic leadership! None were seduced from their loyalty. We only discovered this when the resources ended and the radical elements gave themselves up. The Police Chief and the people were greatly surprised as no one in all the lands had a television.

The satellite television have paid much money for a show to be broadcast from the zoo. We are giving them what they want as this is the modern market economy. At first it was a problem to have both monkeys and tigers, but just one cage. It would require much investment in building and nets. The Minister and the TV have solved these objections. They say it will be like 'Big Brother', but I am unsure as I did not read the classics. The producer is very excited and can sell this show to many countries. The format was as follows:

Day One: Into the tiger's cage there was placed a tree with three branches and four monkeys. This is all filmed to satisfaction.

Day Two: The tiger's cage then has a tree with three branches and three monkeys.
In the night, one of the branches is greased.

Day Three: The cage of many hungry tigers has a tree with two branches and two monkeys. Monkey food is placed on the other side of the compound.

On day four I find that the zoo is closed because of 'International Outcry'. I do not understand this as my country has given you what you asked for. You demand more, then you say it is wrong and Khafui's fault. It is outrageous to see the things Khafui is being called. There are documentary makers writing every day. This is not progress and will be stopped.

The Business Minister has been ironing several fires. The global corporations are agreeing with him for a factory to make rubber running shoes with a little exclamation mark on the side. I asked how much my people are to be paid for this working and it is very little. I ask what the owners are paid and what the shoes sell for. They say it is a different cost of living outside, so the question is irreverent. I am told people will not pay much for shoes in other countries, so if they are not made here very cheaply the factory will have to close and it will all be Khafui's fault. They speak of the Emperor's share options and Greta says this is now a very good deal. I am wise. I am worried for the people. They will have no time to fish now, so are told to spend their new payment on food in the factory shop. It is for convenience and part of progress and regional developments. The foreign investors are speaking of giving them tokens to spend at the shop instead of so much pay. They say this is easier and there will be less tax complications so the share options will be improved and more will be available for Khafui's public generosity. They say more money will be there for hiring policemen.

The Finance Minister is now returned as he is being 'deported'. He advises that this is how the Western Powers say 'to leave a port'. He returns with only some of the money because the rest was taken from him by top investment taxes and many criminal persons. He is very brave and loyal. I will proclaim him with the Order of the Transcrabian Empire at the weekend fish market. There will be most people there this weekend and it will give me some days to find the box these are kept in. The annual winds are much worse this year. They make the dust and the heat move faster. I have heard in the future there will be climate change. I have decided my country should apply for it. Greta will know what to do.

We, Khafui, are a warrior. I have been through the trial of the face painting and the ordeal of the jumping up and down until sunset. The warriors here are very brave. Some mercenaries came years ago when my family lived at the Palace. There was much violence and I was brought home from my educations overseas. It was all gone hideous! The mercenaries had thought this was Belgian Transcrabia, which is all on the mainland of Africa. This is African Transcrabia. There are no Belgians in Africa now. They have all been chased out by the Italian Imperial Forces long ago. The mercenary soldiers were most apologetic and helped with the mending of the damage at no charge. This unpleasantness must never happen again. I have proclaimed all signs and notepaper to carry clear statements to this effect.

I have considered your offer to be represented at the United Nations. I have had letters recognising me. I have written back to these countries which are younger than my empire and I am replying that I am pleased to recognise them too. I sent a map clearly marked which they can pass on to their mercenaries. There are two countries that want to start the war to bring peace and stop aggressive behaviour. There are 167 countries which want to stop this. The two have sent friends to my country and will advise me how to vote. They say I have suffered from violence and must therefore support wars. If I do not, my country will be threatened by warlike people in 45 minutes and it will all be my fault. Two is not enough for international lawfulness. They say a coalition of 3 agreeing countries is same as a majority at the United Nations. Especially if this is wanted by the man who is made President as consolation prize for coming second in the election. At first I said yes, so the new friends went away happy. They were so happy at this news, they forgot to pay their hotel bills. It is most forgetful.

Other African leaders said 'When the sun of integrity is low on the horizon, even the harvest bugs cast long shadows'. I have thought about these words. They are not gracious with respect and I will not have them speak of the Western Powers in this way. They may behave as children now, but with education may grow up as high as the m'gonganut tree. Khafui has changed his mind and will not travel to United Nations. There will be the international coalition anyway. They have found a Spanish man to stand with them and promised him a rock. He is very happy. Maybe they will tell the people who live there. Maybe they are happy too and will be forgetful.

I am worried about the wars of the Western Powers. I am told they have missiles to follow the land and kill the brave man hundreds of miles away as he sleeps. In Sudan such a missile hit the factory making the malaria medicines and many thousands have died. There was no apology or repairing of damage. Perhaps the rubber shoe factory is not such a good idea. Can the missiles read my signs? Will the bravery of my warriors matter if they never see those who attack us? I am wise. I have proclaimed the Minister of Public Works to put lights on the road signs and direct them at the skies. I must hope the bombs are as smart as Khafui.

I have had a correspondence from houseboy's mother, who has gone up in the world and is living in a tower of hamlets. Houseboy's sister has already earned great respect for my country with her modelling in the British newspapers. She is enjoying society and spends much time escorting top politicians at night, whose wives are too busy. It is amazing. She had no interest in opera and theatre when here in Transcrabia. Houseboy's mother has written down the words many honourable politicians say about my country to Houseboy's sister at night. She will write more when the expenses money arrives. I have sent this by return. Houseboy's mother is very, very loyal. She will be my new Minister for Information.

There is much I am to attend to and Greta is of little help and proving most difficult. How many jobs does her boyfriend need? I sometimes miss the girl who did the spitting on the rugs. She would have told me of the submarine in the docks which does not fly my flag. It is all most perplexing. There are no monkeys at the Palace now. The scratching of the insects that live under the roof tiles has become most intolerable at night. I believe the little brown monkeys have been distracted from their loyalty and have done a runner to the docks. Everything has gone hideous.

And now it is that your Attenborough comes.

Yours in serenity,

H.I.M. Kafui I, Emperor in Absolute

THE WORLD THROUGH AN ICE LENS

Part I

Two Eskimos are huddled together in an igloo.
Their names are Harold and Jeremy.
Jeremy is a girl.

Jeremy: "Why are they called Harp Seals anyway?"

Harold: "I think they're sponsored by a lager company."

Jeremy: "What for?"

Harold: "They thought it might appeal to people who go clubbing."

Jeremy: "It's pathetic when you think about it. We've got four hundred traditional words to describe snow, and only one traditional joke. I hate being an Eskimo."

Harold: "That's why you've got a southern name. It gives you broad horizons."

Jeremy: "Why Jeremy though? Why can't I have a girls name?"

Harold: "It's obvious. This is a very harsh environment. The Elders didn't want to give any of the other Eskimos a reason to take their clothes off."

Jeremy: "Remember the hut those explorers built last summer? I went up there today. They'd left bits of newspaper all over the floor with stuff about the outside world. I should have written down some of it, only my hands were too cold. Anyway, it started me thinking, I want to have a girl's name like that Sharon who runs Israel."

Harold: "You can get easily distracted by some of these strange foreign notions. Apparently, Ireland's run by a tea shop. The explorers left this hardware catalogue when they went. It said 'P&Q will deliver to your home address for a £5 flat rate'. That could be useful to us, except we haven't got any money. P&Q, I wonder where they are?"

Jeremy: "Probably from one of those countries down south."

Harold: "All countries are down south dear."

Jeremy: "I saw a polar bear lob a seal over it's own head today. Wind assisted mind."

Harold: "That's nothing. I found some snow with little fizzing holes in it where the huskies had been. It looked just like a Damien Hurst dot painting."

Jeremy: "Better, I would have thought."

Harold: "I'm bored. That's the trouble with having our new global outlook. The snow is always cleaner on the other side. Less huskies evacuating themselves in it for a start."

Jeremy: "Why don't we play one of the traditional games?"

Harold: "Tell me about that one where you pin the tail on the narwhal."

Jeremy: "That's really just for the tourists. You boil a polar bear's leg bone until it goes soft, pull and twist it, then cool it down and sharpen the end. Let the pot carry on boiling until it turns into gloopy glue, then dip the stumpy end in. After that, it's just a matter of waiting until a pilot whale sticks it's head up through a hole in the ice, then…"

Harold: "Plop it on his nose, instant narwhal, laugh yourself silly 'till sunrise."

Jeremy: "Which is five months away."

Harold: "I suppose we'll forget all the old ways now we're globalising society."

Jeremy: "I don't see why we have to globalise."

Harold: "Global shrinking."

Jeremy: "What?"

Harold: "When the world gets warmer, the ice melts, then the arctic ice cap gets smaller and smaller. Shrinking, see? Our world gets smaller. Could suit us of course. Property prices will have to go up. Then, eventually, you have to sell before property goes down. Suddenly. All the way to the bottom of the sea."

Jeremy: "That's a long way off yet though. It's still a bit nippy out."

Harold's finger nail has just turned black and fallen off.

He looks at it dejectedly.

Harold: "I Suppose you're right dear."

[Exeunt]

Part II

Two Eskimos are energetically bashing a frozen ice hole with ineffective bone clubs.

For a minute and a half they furiously smash, bash and thud their way into the top half an inch of ice. Thump, bash, club, wump, wallop, bash, bash, bash, bash.

A seal pops up through a completely different ice hole, out of their eye-line, and waddles towards them to see what all the fuss is about.

The Eskimos eventually grind to a halt, exhausted.

There is a significant pause.

The Eskimos see the seal.

They gradually stand up in a stealthy manner, then grab their clubs and run toward it yelling "aaaaaaaarrrrrrhhhhh."

The seal's eyes widen, it backs up and slips down the ice hole.

The Eskimos arrive and stare down the hole, defeated.

Some time later…

Harold enters the igloo, pulls off his glove and his finger falls off.

He stares at it dejectedly.

He looks up at Jeremy.

Harold: "Bit nippy out."

[Exeunt]

Part III

A group of Eskimos are sitting on a mound of snow watching a lone polar explorer painfully dragging his sled along in the far distance.

The Eskimos are eating strips of dried meat, in the manner of a cinema audience.

The explorer keeps glancing in their direction, as if wondering what they want.

There is a significant pause, punctuated by the sound of a dragging sled.

Out of nowhere, a huge white bear pounces and smothers the explorer and both disappear from view behind a snowdrift.

The Eskimos applaud briefly and get back to their chores.

Some time later…

Harold drags the explorer's sled to a stop outside the igloo.

It appears to have half a pilot whale on top of it.

Jeremy: "Any fish today dear?"

Harold: "Look for yourself."

Jeremy looks outside. There is a significant pause.

Jeremy: "They're going to want that back you know."

[Exeunt]

Part IV

An Eskimo stands over an ice hole with a hatchet held poised above his head.

He has been there a very long time.

An icicle has formed on his nose.

There is another significant wait.

A seal's head pops through the ice.

The Eskimo topples over backwards, completely frozen in position.

Some time later…

Harold is thawing out beside a whale-fat fire in the igloo.

Eventually his mouth twitches and moves.

Part of Harold's frostbitten left ear falls off.

He stares at it dejectedly.

Harold: "Bit nippy out."

[Exeunt]

Part V

Two Eskimos are fishing in an ice hole. They are very quiet and concentrate fiercely.

Some way off, the ice groans and cracks. A submarine turret rises through the surface.

The hatch opens and a figure trudges toward them through the endless carpet of snow.

He fidgets around them for a while, wondering what to say.

One Eskimo says to another, subtitled in Inuit, "Just ignore him."

There is a significant pause.

In Inuit again: "If he asks for directions, tell him to go south."

Submariner: "Hello lads. Caught anything?"

There is a significant pause while the Eskimos ignore him.

The submariner looks non-plussed.

There is a slight icy cracking noise.

One of Harold's eyebrows falls off.

Submariner: "Bit nippy out."

He trudges back to the conning tower, closes the hatch and the boat submerges.

[Exeunt]

Part VI

An Eskimo stands over an ice hole with a hatchet held poised above his head.

He has been there a very long time.

An icicle has formed on his nose.

There is another significant wait.

He slowly focuses on two hairy white legs on the other side of the ice hole.

To the accompaniment of a slight cracking noise from his neck, the head raises up to look at what's in front of him. It is a polar bear.

There is a significant pause.

The Eskimo dives down the ice hole.

The polar bear adopts exactly the position the Eskimo had been waiting in.

Some time later…

Harold enters the igloo, pulls off his boot and a selection of toes fall off.
He stares at what's left of his foot dejectedly. He looks up at Jeremy.

Harold: "Bit nippy out."

Jeremy stares at him.

Jeremy: "No fish today then dear?"

Harold doesn't answer.

Jeremy looks blank. "I thought you were going to get that seen to."

[Exeunt]

Part VII

Harold enters the igloo. He sounds mildly inebriated.

Harold [reciting]:

> "Icelandic people live in fear
> of the one they call Bruce the Queer.
> Icelandic farmers live in dread
> 'cos old Bruce takes sheep to bed.
>
> Codfish, haddock, whitefish, skate.
> They use their tails for fishing bait,
> but Icelandic folk I've never known
> Would not deign to fish alone…"

Harold accidentally knocks over some paddles and a harpoon which were neatly stacked against the wall. They clatter to the floor.

There is a significant pause.

Jeremy: "That's from a fine old traditional Icelandic Saga, is it?"

Harold: "Pretty much. At least that's the way they told it in that pub in Greenland."

Jeremy: "Yes, well. Greenlanders are no better than they ought to be, and you're drunk. It's shameful."

After another pause.

Jeremy: "Um, how does the saga end?"

Harold: "Chillingly."

Harold starts packing clothes.

Harold: "After that there was a bit of a fight. Lucky I took my club."

Jeremy: "Where are you off to then?"

Harold: "Alaska, maybe Canada."

Jeremy: "What? You can't leave!"

Harold doesn't respond, pauses in thought, then continues packing.

Jeremy: "Who will I have to talk to?"

Harold: "I'm going to work on one of those ships that hoover up all the salmon in the ocean to make catfood. When there are no salmon left I'll probably go south again, to Nova Scotia. I might even become a singer-songwriter like cousin Bjerk."

Jeremy: "Oh Harold, you can't go to Canada. There's hardly any ice. Do you know what the heat's like there? About minus one. You'll fry! Your coat will shrink and you'll never get out. What happens if you hole your canoe on a cacti?"

Harold: "What's the first rule of Eskimo society? Think, Jeremy. What's the one thing the Elders have always instilled into our national consciousness?"

Jeremy: "That's easy. Never, ever, take your coat off."

They pause, significantly.

Jeremy: "So what are you going to do?"

Harold: "The world's changing dear. We can't just sit here avoiding it any more. I'm going south. I'm going to… TAKE MY COAT OFF!"

Jeremy: "Not just yet dear. It's still a bit nippy out."

Cue pointless dancing girls wearing furry hats.

They jostle to get into the front row.

One at the back is briefly seen to be holding a fluffy toy polar bear, which she drops.

[Exeunt]

ST. DUNSTAN'S ISLAND

Cast of characters

Crispin Campbell public servant and career political animal.
Josiah Trescothick bewildered Cornish carpenter.
Tristan Campbell's secretary and general voice on the phone.

Clearly in an alternative reality, many, many years from now…
In the office of the Minister for Social Injustice, London:

Campbell: "Now, Trescothick is it?"

Trescothick: "Sir."

Campbell: "Allergic to coconuts?"

Trescothick: "No Sir. I don't think so."

Campbell: "You may have been wondering why you've been brought here."

Trescothick: "Rounded up and dragged off by the Police, yes. They treated us worse than the Scrumpy Festival of '98, and we hadn't done anything this time. You can't just go round havin' people arrested!"

Campbell: "You were detained in a legitimate fact-finding exercise to establish the identities of unregistered migrants, or 'trans-nationals', as we say in Whitehall."

Trescothick: "Yes, but I'm not one of them immigrants, see. I'm Cornish!"

Campbell: "Is that the truth though, or is it just what they wanted you to believe?"

Trescothick: "I don't quite follow Sir."

Campbell: "You see, well I suppose someone has to tell you sooner or later… You're Polynesian."

Trescothick: "Can't be!"

Campbell: "Alright. I realise this has come as something of a shock to you, but consider the evidence. For example, have you noticed that your accent is different to other people's?"

Trescothick: "Everyone speaks like that in my part of Cornwall."

Campbell: "Interesting, yes interesting. A whole community of Polynesian colonists living undetected in Cornwall. I wonder what the Cabinet will say when they find out. It won't be a pretty sight, but then again it never is. Well, I'm sorry to break it to you, but we've decided to take action."

Trescothick: "I see Sir. So what are you going to do about it?"

Campbell: "Well, as you are no doubt aware, Britain is rather overcrowded at the moment. Indeed, it's reached a stage where some of my London friends don't even have a second home in Cornwall. I'm sure none of us want to see this alarming situation persist, so to cut a long story short, we're sending you back. To the Peloponnese that is."

Trescothick: "I thought you said Polynesia?"

Campbell: "Ah, I'm afraid you've fallen for my deliberate trap. You know slightly too much about it already don't you? No good denying it now of course, wheels in motion, unread reports to file. Yes, yes, you're quite right. Her Majesty's Government is sending you back to Polynesia. We've checked the archives and found a remote British Territory called St.Dunstan's Island which could use some new blood. It's a bit like Agalega and the Chagos Archipelago, only less well known."

Trescothick: "You can't! I pay my taxes!"

Campbell: "Really? How wonderfully naive."

Trescothick: "What do you mean?"

Campbell: "Nothing. Rather late to introduce you to my accountant anyway, now you're off."

Trescothick: "But, where…?"

Campbell: "To the South Seas apparently. Not appearing on my globe, but don't worry – the captain will know where you're going if your parents can't remember. You're a carpenter by trade aren't you?"

Trescothick: "Yes Sir. So was my father and my father's father."

Campbell: "Should know all about canoes and outriggers then. That'll be a handy head start for you."

Trescothick: "Are there many trees on the island then Sir?"

[Campbell leans forward, adopting a reassuring tone]

Campbell: "We have no indication that it isn't an arboreal paradise. Possibly because we've mislaid the file, but I expect there are other, more convincing, reasons too."

Trescothick: "If I'm losing my house, will there be compensation?"

Campbell: "HMG is trying not to set a precedent on that one. Nothing personal, but otherwise we might be letting ourselves in for a hell of a bill when we offload Gibraltar."

Trescothick: "Won't people object?"

Campbell: "Not really. That's the power of the focus group. We ask a room full of colonial locals how they would answer a hypothetical question like "Would you approve of your land being given to another country as a bribe for their support in the UN?" Re-phrased of course. It was originally called the Diego Garcia Ploy. If they come up with an answer we don't like, we simply don't ask the question. It's then just a matter of saying people were 'crying out for it all along'. If you say something like that often enough, it becomes the truth, at least as far as the history books are concerned. How do you think we joined the PEU?"

Trescothick: "I see. Public service is more complicated than I thought."

Campbell: "You don't know the half of it, and I expect you wouldn't believe me if you did. There are some times when you simply can't let the public know things. That's what the restricted section of the Freedom of Information Act is all about. About 30% of the overall document, or so I'm told. Not allowed to see it myself"

Trescothick: "What document is that then? I hadn't heard about it."

Campbell: "As I say, there are some things the populace don't need to know. For instance, did you think we changed the coins every three years just to keep the Royal portrait updated? It's all a cunning plan to get shot of our excess nuclear fuel waste. We put a tiny blip of depleted uranium in each new coin minted and people just queue up to take it away! Why do you think bank vaults are lead-lined? We even let countries pay us to accept spent fuel rods because we've got a magical system for 'reprocessing' them. Wonderful really. That's the real reason the Government's so keen to impose the peuro. We could then seed our radioactive material all over the continent! It would be much safer if we spread it out over a wider area. Of course, tax would be a problem. Naturally, we'd prefer people to now 'pay unto Caesar' by direct debit."

Trescothick: "But Sir, wouldn't people get sick?"

Campbell: "That's hardly a problem. It's just a matter of blaming the side effects on mobile phones. Anyway, just consider the advantages: If anyone attempted to approach a bank with lots of them, our satellite sensors in orbit would pick up the signal of concentrated radiation and warn the bank. Just as the customer approaches the little cashier's window trying to change them for a more stable currency, they can pull down the little blind which says 'Closed' or 'Fermé', refuse to accept them back, and also do their bit to reduce devaluation.

Perhaps you may have noticed that trials of this system have already been staged? Usually at lunch-time when the most people are trying to pay in. The preliminary tests with the little magnetic strips on railway tickets were generally less successful, but I think we have a winner this time."

Trescothick: "It won't work. I dunno anyone who wants to drop the pound. People won't accept it if you don't bother to ask them."

Campbell: "Ah, we've thought of that. Do you remember the election where we said 'this is NOT a referendum about giving the country away, this is an election to choose your representative for

Parliament'. Then, after winning, we said 'this result proves once and for all that the public are dead keen to have their opinions on the PEU roundly ignored and leave everything to us'? Perhaps you remember that old chestnut 'would you like to trade with other countries in a common market?' Ha-ha! Just to be sure, we're going to let all PEU citizens visiting here vote in our referendum. The plan is to ship millions of them over in barges from Gdansk, then in return we'll pay for their economic failures."

Trescothick: "Yes, I just about remember. It all rushed by so fast I couldn't take it all in. Is that what they call spin doctoring? I've often wondered."

Campbell: "The original idea was to have a referendum which asked a completely different question. One where the only answers provided to choose from suited us anyway. We considered having a vote on something vaguely related such as 'should we surrender our economy a) now, or b) next Tuesday', which could retrospectively be cited as proof the public have full confidence in all Government policies, in general. Er, even the ones we haven't thought of yet. Now, the spin-doctors have come up with a better idea than that. The new Government solution is to ring the front doorbell, ask the householder a completely different question, then have someone slip the peuros in by the back door. We just hope they're headed out of the room when they turn the light off that evening as the new coins do have a rather unfortunate residual radioactive glow."

Trescothick: "Like those luminous stars they put in children's bedrooms?"

Campbell: "What an excellent idea! I feel a memo to Research & Development coming on. I can see you're going to be quite a loss after all. It really is amazing, given that it's your first trip to London."

Trescothick: "Can I ask you a question?"

Campbell: "Of course you can. It's a free country. At least, I assume Phase Four isn't ahead of schedule. It's often hard to be open about these things to the general public. They can be so obstructive. It's good to have someone like you to talk to; someone who won't be around much longer. Sorry, you were saying?"

Trescothick: "Why's it called St.Dunstan's then?"

Campbell: "When the Royal Navy ran aground, sorry, discovered it during one of their usual forays around the region, the captain had already come up with names for 110 Micronesian islands and was then understandably at a bit of a loss. A crewman suggested 'Dunstan' as the youngest of Queen Victoria's sixty grandchildren and the captain duly obliged. On later investigation by a specialist tour operator, ah yes Tropical & Wilderness Survival Tours of Grimsby…"

Trescothick: "Wilderness?"

Campbell: " 'Wilderness' being the Afrikaans word for 'bountiful'. On investigation it was established that none of Queen Victoria's grandchildren were in fact called Dunstan and it seems more likely to have been the name of the ship's goat. This may also explain the instances of monolithic goat-like effigies spotted over the years by passing vessels. In the mid sixties the F.O. amended it to 'St.Dunstan's' as that seems to cover all eventualities."

Trescothick: "Didn't anyone notice?"

Campbell: "I really don't think they've ever had it on headed paper before."

Trescothick: "Why are you reading all this from a travel brochure?"

Campbell: "I'm just soaking up the gorgeous atmosphere of the place whilst we have this little chat. I wouldn't be over concerned with the details if I were you. These little colonies are usually fairly civilised. I understand the last official communication said they're still loyal to King & Country."

Trescothick: "King Sir?"

Campbell: "It's the provinces. The Government doesn't care about anything outside London, so they're probably a little out of touch. I'm told a similar copy was sent to the King of Australia, but that may have been an elaborate joke."

Trescothick: "Australia Sir?"

Campbell: "No Trescothick. Where was I? Although distant, they're still loyal and that's the main thing. When they heard, a platoon of St.Dunstinians was despatched to aid the motherland in World War II. Of course the poor dears arrived in the 60s and we thought they were from Guadeloupe, but that was okay – we used them at Suez. Still there for all I know. *[pushes buzzer]* Tristan? Be a good lad and check if those provincial irregulars are still drawing army pay would you? Should give some indication where they've got to. We could always cancel their pension. That would get them writing in. Unless their English isn't very clear or they don't live near a post office. We saved a bundle that way with the Gurkhas."

Trescothick: "How many people live there?"

Australis Ambernectoris-Larrikini Ringpullissimo Rex

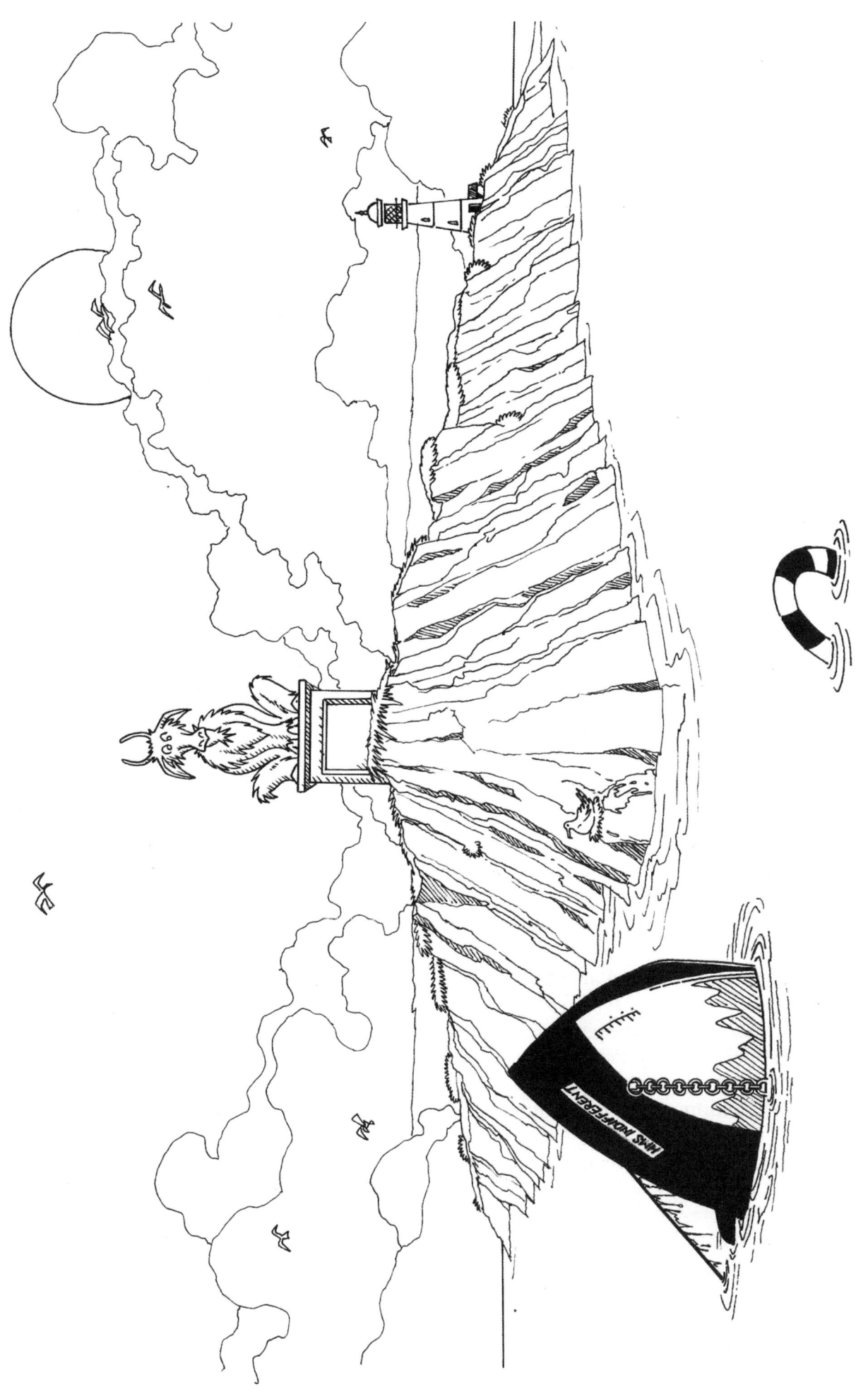

Campbell: "Well, indeed. How many do live there? Now it's funny you should dredge that one up as it's been the subject of some speculation around the office and, well, we were hoping you could tell us. An estimate would be fine. After all, that's all we had for the Falklands in '82."

Trescothick: "Is it a democracy then? Like Britain?"

Campbell: "Are you referring to the highest form of political power? Well, of course Britain's ruled by the Peuropean Commission, an entirely unelected foreign government, so things aren't always what they seem. The PEU has so far ended democracy as the highest form of political power in all 25 member countries. That's more effective than Fascism and Communism combined! Of course, the PM knows that the public get upset by strange Greek words like 'tyranny', so we prefer to gloss over the subject wherever possible. I don't know why we bother."

Trescothick: "Isn't any of that stuff illegal? I can't believe they clobbered us good and proper at the Scrumpy Festival and that was going on at the same time."

Campbell: "Ratifying the Haastricht treaty did break the Magna Carta, subjugate the Monarch and end democracy. It's not as though you can complain to the highest court in our land, because the highest court is no longer in our land. It's the PEU court. Over-ruled! Checkmate! Just to be on the safe side, the Government quietly did away with the death penalty for High Treason. Can't have any busybodies getting lucky, can we?"

Trescothick: "I'm going to complain about all this to the PM!"

Campbell: "Prime Minister Deptford-Twang? The man who keeps us in the PEU, against the wishes of over two thirds of the population? The man who started a war with the support of just 18% of the public? The Japanese President's noodle? Face it Trescothick; It's hardly likely he'll listen to you. When he wants your opinion, he'll tell you what it is."

Trescothick: "There must be something we can do?"

Campbell: "The system's been designed so you can't. That's the first secret they let you in on in the modern Plabour party. The Ptories and Pliberals are in on it too. If you've got the politicians in your back pocket, it makes conquering countries so much easier than all that 'so last century' dressing up in uniforms and shouting nonsense."

Trescothick: "Surely, you mean Labour and the place gettin' run by the EU?"

Campbell: "No similarity whatsoever. I'm surprised you'd even make the association. It would take a real alternative reality for any Prime Minister to be arrogant and power-crazed enough to take the P."

Trescothick: "Oh. I suppose I'd better get used to it then."

Campbell: "Good lad. That's the spirit. Make a Philippino or whatever out of you yet. Adaptability. It's all part of the new world order they keep banging on about. It's like freedom. The PM is rather keen to phase out the 'F' word and shift the emphasis more toward 'duty to the leader'. Democracy is all very well, but it's so much more efficient when the public aren't getting in the way, fouling things up all the time."

Trescothick: "You make it sound like those ruddy machine people from Star Truck! 'Your opinion is irrelevant. Democracy is irrelevant. You have been assimilated'. You've got me in such a state I won't be gettin' any sleep what with worryin'."

Campbell: "Quite. Unless, of course, you're lucky enough to be taking the next boat to a tropical paradise… I'd love to tag along, but I can't. Someone has to stay here and supervise the sinking ship. Slip of the tongue. I mean, of course, 'transition period'. If I were you, I'd get out of here while the going's good. You're one of 'The Public'. Decisions won't be made in the interests of 'The Public' any more. We're trying something new. We've got… The Project."

Trescothick: "But we have elections!"

Campbell: "Yes. Distracting isn't it? A lovely little attention grabber. Sadly, the politicians who rule the country can't spare the time to get elected. Brussels is such a busy place nowadays. I remember one of the Chancellors of the Exchequer won a fortune at the bookies on that particular outsider at the time. Bet the public wouldn't notice. Lost it all on the 2,000 Guineas a week later, so it didn't do him much good. At least, until his state pay-off came through after that mix up losing our national pension reserves chasing his losses on the exchange rate mechanism. Always fun to bet with other people's money. Especially if you're a bit 'compulsive'."

Trescothick: "I've noticed you don't always answer the question. I can't be sure where you stand at all and it's not easy seeing what's going on when you lot are being so evasive. I mean, I know you're working in our best interests…"

Campbell: "Excuse my blushes. Oh, thank you so much. It's little comments like that which make my humble day worthwhile. You really should meet my number-crunchers. They've got a rather impolite acronym for members of the electorate in your category. Until now, it was my understanding your sort were purely theoretical. Apparently, the PM's been dying to meet one. He's got a second hand car he's always trying to sell and none of his colleagues seem interested."

Campbell: "Correct me if I'm wrong, but you don't appear to be the sort of person who'd vote for my party."

Trescothick: "No, and I won't again after your lot closed our local hospital and sold our village graveyard to that supermarket for ten ruddy pence! Our postman's granny is buried under a freezer full of mechanically recovered chicken nuggets!"

Campbell: "Not smart backing the wrong side in a key-marginal is it?"

Trescothick: "I always thought them MPs were meant to speak up for the interests of the people who sent them? Represent their constituency, that sort of thing. Not just get told how to vote by their party. They're representatives of the people. Aren't they?"

Campbell: "Good Lord, no. We had enough trouble containing that sort of nonsense with Gandhi! What the public want is a politician with such self-belief and vision that he's prepared to bet your life on it. 'On one turn of pitch and toss' as they say. Almost all politicians nowadays are effectively pitching tossers."

Trescothick: "What if the public protest?"

Campbell: "Easy – If they get too close to the mark, we simply stir up a conflict with the most convenient tin-pot country and declare a state of emergency. If anyone criticises the government in a time of war, they are clearly a traitor and we can round them up too. If they're patriotic we just think of a demeaning name for them like 'Little Englander', deploy it in the weekly soundbytes, and Bob's your uncle – loyalty is the new radicalism. If a modern politician hears the words 'principles', 'nation' or 'patriot' they write a speech for the devolver."

[an intercom buzzes, followed by a muffled voice]

Tristan: "The Under-Secretary for Contempt is on the line wondering if you've got another for him. Something else about progress on 'Operation Lowland Clearance'."

Campbell: "Tell Tolemy… or is it Ptolemy? I always get those mixed up. Tell him I'll call back in an hour will you? The usual arrangements."

Trescothick: "Is St Dunstan's Island a democracy then? Do you know anything about the place?"

Campbell: "Administration for the more far-flung specks of pink is run through an old weather computer in our Hobart office. St.Dunstans has only one officially recorded voter since, at the last census, Hurricane Aleé appears to be the only name the computer knew for sure was in the region. I'm afraid the poor thing's junk mail has been mis-directed to Pitcairn ever since, where I hear it's causing some degree of upset. You see, they're afraid that one day it may decide to come and collect the post."

Trescothick: "Bit primitive are they Sir?"

Campbell: "The Post Office has made great strides and it's not for us to criticise. Maybe you're just the chap to show us all how it's done. When you do become the Numero-Uno in the region, be sure to let us know and perhaps we can mint some currency for you."

Trescothick: "Should be fine with the Cowrie shells Sir."

Campbell: "Be a good lad then, and remember to give blood before you go. After all, we've taken just about everything else."

Trescothick: "Sorry?"

[the intercom buzzes again]

Tristan: "Prime Minister Deptford-Twang's on the line. He's asking if you can clear some more locals out of Tuscany. He's found another spot he quite fancies."

Campbell: "Put him on hold. He's not very important any more."

Trescothick: "What's all this about Tuscany?"

Campbell: "Returning to my original point, perhaps you could manage a quick head-count when they drop you off. An estimate really, before the ship leaves, since there may not be another opportunity for some time. You never know though. It might be worth our trouble fining them for not being registered to vote!"

Trescothick: "But Sir!"

Campbell: "Oh, don't fuss. You'll make lots of new friends. When the atmospheric conditions are right, you can probably make radio contact with the tiny colony on Tinker's Island. They're English speakers. Well, it's a kind of English. We had to deport them from Docklands in the early eighties. No, don't thank me. Just run along and pack your things. On your way out, Tristan will give you the Ministry's approved pamphlet on the care of the goat. Leave your door keys under the mat. Try to persuade as many of your friends as possible to report themselves before the ship sails, and Trescothick…"

Trescothick: "Sir?"

Campbell: "No sneaky teaching your children cricket and rugger, then sending them back to haunt us."

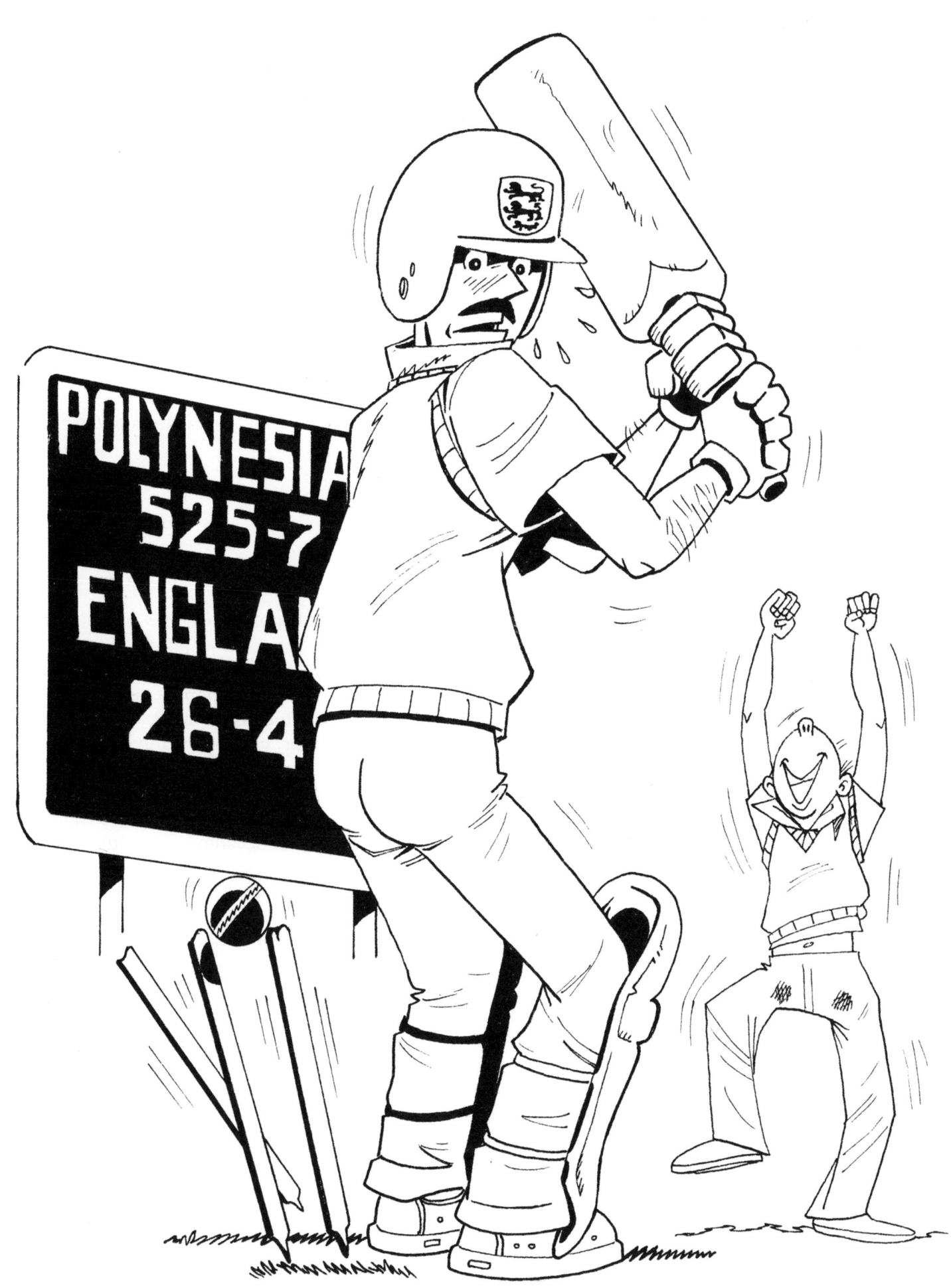

DUBIOUS COMPANY

(a.k.a. The National Society for the Propagation & Dissemination of Rumours)

Cast of characters

Sir Terrence Bunsen tree surgeon and ex-managing director
Alec standard bearer of the national Youth Training Scheme

A rotund and burly tree surgeon, together with his young and freckly assistant, are slowly working their way up a majestic tree, cutting bits off as they go…

Alec: "Been a tree surgeon long?"

Sir Terrence: "Not really. It's my first day."

Alec: "Hang on. You hired me. Your name's written on the van! Right above the words 'Tree Surgeon'."

Sir Terrence: "You really don't understand the first principle of aspirational management do you? How do you expect to get work if you start off by telling people you can't do it? People see what they expect to see, so if you say you're worth forty pounds an hour, you'll probably get it. Have you ever heard of computer troubleshooting? Football transfers?"

Alec: "Okay, I can see that, but if we know the same amount about it, um, how come you're training me? Why, in fact, do I have to accept lower wages during my apprenticeship? Come to think of it, why are you the boss?"

Sir Terrence: "First thing you've got to learn when you set up a business is to take responsibility for personnel. It's the best position to be in when you want to make sure you've got yourself the best job. When you're being interviewed for the managing director role, it's vital being in a position to control the opposition."

Alec: "Other companies?"

Sir Terrence: "No, I mean deciding who else gets invited to the interview. I couldn't do your job you see? I'm the sort of person who just naturally gravitates to the top of the tree. You're what would be described as the workforce; people traditionally forced to work. I only really hired you to make a naff joke about having Alec to stand on."

Alec: "That's an odd way of looking at it. I thought we were doing exactly the same thing, just cutting branches."

Sir Terrence: "That takes me back. My job at the bank mostly involved cutting branches. It's all changed now though. I went back to my old town recently and I couldn't believe it. One look at the high street and I thought "Oh, my God! My trendy wine bar's become a bank!" All that good work undone at a fleabitten stroke."

Alec: "So you were a sort of messenger, going from head office out to the regional branches?"

Sir Terrence: "More a sort of harbinger. Interesting word. It's almost irresistible to add the word 'doom' afterwards."

Alec: "So your job was to make people worried their jobs weren't safe and generally mess them about to make them work harder?"

Sir Terrence: "Survival of the fittest is perfectly natural you know. It's the same principle as replacing a perfectly good skilled worker with two untrained new ones, on a quarter of the salary, and telling them the one who's best at the job gets to stay on. It doesn't work for long of course. It's no use repeatedly manipulating other people. They get fed up with it and leave, then sooner or later you end up on your own just manipulating yourself. That's not a healthy business in the long run."

Alec: "I thought you worked for a big corporation. What was it called? Coagulated Enterprises?"

Sir Terrence: "British Allied Unlimited Conglomerated Aggregated Enterprises Plc. They tried changing it to a vacuous unpatented name with no established connotations, but the only ones left were 'Consignia', 'Snickers' and 'Ka'. They soon got snapped up. I drafted a memo proposing 'Atlantiscibe', but someone pointed out it's already a brand of cuttlefish-based hacksaw lubricant from Catalonia and means 'tragic nodule' in Esperanto. I can't bring myself to explain what the phrase 'hypoallergenic aquaspheres' means in Swahili. Quite disgusting. It became Coagulated Enterprises later. Ah! Diving into the glorious moneypit of private health care. When it gets too expensive for the average person, just think of the new pastures crying out for exploitation. Have you considered the latest opportunities in DIY dentistry?"

Alec: "Then I'm guessing you chucked it all in for tree surgery after some sort of mid-life crisis. What happened? I expect your wife left you, or you went to a party at the CEO of Ergonomic Frameworks Plc and just couldn't compete with the depth of pile in his carpet. That's what it all comes down to isn't it? People taking you seriously at work and then the occasional silly game of one-upmanship?"

Sir Terrence: "Blast it all!"

Alec: "What's wrong? Knob too small?"

Sir Terrence: "There isn't a knob on this chainsaw. It's a kind of starter cord. Just pass me the other one will you? Thanks. Yes, this works fine. Watch out below! We'll soon be through the last of these branches. No, you don't understand the background. I wasn't one of those fat cats you read about in your greasy tabloids. I was the victim of a conspiracy."

Alec: "You're kidding? There's something out there even more ruthless than your corporation? Unlikely."

Sir Terrence: "Oh, there is and you don't know the half of it. It's a power which has brought down businesses…"

Alec: "Don't tell me, you've probably come up with this to avoid taking the blame for bringing Flitish Airlines to it's knees with your trendy new management style. Weren't half your middle managers hospitalised with botulism following that 'group rough and hug it' weekend in rural Mexico?"

Sir Terrence: "It was 'Group hug & rough it', actually."

Alec: "Then you said you didn't want to be the national carrier any more because you're a 'world carrier' and have no loyalty to an individual country, especially for tax purposes, and instantly downsized your most loyal customer base just before bonus time. Even got rid of the flag. I'm sure it was you that decided you were going to paint your logo on sturgeons tails instead and lost a dozen promising executives when the raft they'd built drifted out into the Barents Sea and got landed on by an Ekranoplan. Some improvement that was! Very funny though. The press loved it."

Sir Terrence: "'Improvement'. Ah, that would be a value-laden term. I turned that company around. I was clearly the best person in it, even though I cultivated my down to earth image. My PA spent hours every morning ironing designer creases into my shirt. It's hardly my fault the place worked on an incentive scheme. Golden goodbyes. If you do badly enough, they soon pay you a few million to go away. I suspect it's the same sort of deal they offer the politicians."

Alec: "I've figured that we're lopping the branches off first so the whole canopy falling won't hit those buildings, but why are we cutting this tree down anyway? It doesn't look diseased. Is there going to be a housing development or something?"

Sir Terrence: "Nothing planned, no. It's just that someone told the owner that the tree was a fine example of it's kind. A really beautiful tree. The landowner was so proud. The landowner thought about it. The tree had to go. You see, if the council had noticed how beautiful it was and put a 'tree preservation order' on it, development would be ruled out in the future. This tree is clearly worthy of protection and therefore must be cut down rather than risk a devaluation of the land's potential worth. Simple economics, and I'm here to exploit it. In terms of cash per hour, tree surgery is one of the best jobs in the country."

Alec: "You're lower than badger tackle, aren't you?"

Sir Terrence: "You over-estimate their ability at rugby."

Alec: "The branches are getting thinner up here aren't they? Just twigs really. They keep snapping off. Just a second. Why didn't we start cutting the branches at the top of the tree and work our way down?"

Sir Terrence: "Simple business principle. Never take an action which positions you in the firing line. The best way to get ahead is to keep your head down. If we had cut the branches at the top first, they'd fall towards us on their way to the ground. Obvious. You don't need any training to see that do you?"

Alec: "Yes, but instead, we've cut away all the branches on the way up and are at the top of the tree, unable to get back down. Is this something to do with tackling one problem at a time, or shall I shout until someone gets the fire brigade?"

Sir Terrence: "If there's one thing I've learned a thousand times in business, it's that disasters open up new opportunities. Now I'll have plenty of time to tell you that story."

Alec: "Is this the unlikely conspiracy story, the ekranoplan, or the one about hugging roughage?"

Sir Terrence: "The conspiracy of course. The reason why I'm here!"

Alec: "Apart from the forty pounds an hour? Sorry, you were saying?"

Sir Terrence: "It's a power which has brought down businesses… princes, nations and restaurants with dubious hygiene standards. It's a power which can be found all around us, poisoning offices and workplaces across the planet. It's an invisible assassin, fast as buckshot and everyone, everyone, is vulnerable."

Alec: "Cool. Where can I get some?"

Sir Terrence: "As everyone knows, British Allied was going through a pretty rocky ride this time last year, so I was on a trip to negotiate selling it to the Koreans at a knock down price. Then I made my fatal mistake. I sent round a memo announcing I knew all about the rumours and I'd be putting a stop to it as soon as I got back. As part of the standard corporate package of twenty weeks paid leave, I decided I'd have a bit of a holiday before the negotiations. In Asia they like to negotiate over meals, so I needed to firm up my banqueting muscles.

As soon as I was gone, the chatter started. What I hadn't realised was that my office, my business, was simply a front for the most devious and insidious parasite the business world has ever known. That's right! The British Allied building was also the headquarters of… The National Society for the Propagation & Dissemination of Rumours!"

Alec: "What? Someone organises that stuff? It would certainly explain all that bilge about the moon landings being faked because the shadows don't match up. Pathetic. Hank wasn't even an astronaut."

Sir Terrence: "Quite. Anyway, they couldn't take the chance you see? They thought I was on to them. I had to go. It bagan with the spam emails. Carefully worded and disseminated to their dedicated team of office workers worldwide. Alienating, malicious, personal and with an uncanny amount of speculation on matters of my medical history. It even went as far as where I go to get the little blue pills. It's never extended that far before. I hate rumours because I can't control them. They go around the world in a flash. Several other chief executives forwarded them back to me for verification. I wasn't there of course, so they looked pretty true."

Alec: "What did they say? I expect it was pretty hot stuff. I heard a good one the other day about the Bishop of Falkirk. It didn't sound that likely though. You'd never get the right sort of extension lead."

Sir Terrence: "Ah, the gist, the nub. Yes, well they speculated that my private jet had crashed into a small uninhabited island in the waters of a South East Asian nation which would not allow foreign search vessels to approach. Some smart-alec tabloid even reported that my jet had flown into a solid cloud. They said there were 'questions' over the pension fund. After a while, the rumour grew. The world of finance operates entirely on rumours, so at the first sniff of a rat there was a run on the shares, contracts were cancelled and every single executive on the board jumped ship. Gutless, the lot of them.

It was then, they said, the junior staff started to run the company. Miss Flipley, one of the senior secretaries, assumed control and started appointing new directors. She spends a lot of time with

that Balkan oddity who does my typing. It's almost as if Flipley was taking orders from her. The first meeting was a little strange. There was a report on research and product development from the newly appointed director of abstract design. I doubt he even knew he was meant to be in a meeting. You see, he'd been loitering around the reception desk with his tennis clothes on, absentmindedly thumping yellow balls into the portrait of a Managing Director 1923-1927, waiting for Miss Surnameescapesme. Flipley arrived and pushed him into the meeting. When the other directors asked him for a report, he began by sporting the expression of a man who's just been asked to recite Kubla Khan backwards.

He looked a bit blank then, to begin with, as these clever technical chappies so often do, but soon cottoned on that something was expected of him. The presentation was apparently an astounding feat of hybrid design. He pulled out what at first appeared, to all the shallow fools in the room, to be an ordinary tennis ball. A-ha, he explained, that's just to throw the corporate espionage fellows off the scent! It's actually a prototype for a highly advanced digital video-phone/fax/computer/oven/parachute/ highland rescue compact terminal, which can be made using incredibly advanced lightweight technology to be almost the exact weight, texture and appearance of a standard tennis ball. It's so sturdy, you can even bounce it off the wall! He demonstrated by neatly pummelling a portrait of the founder, 1899-1913, on the far side of the complimentary mineral water. A glass fell over.

Of course, he said, to make it really realistic it's just a matter of taking out the internal workings, as with this prototype. The safe version is also guaranteed not to electrocute damp golden retrievers. This modification also saves on costs, doesn't have the irritating little ringtone and can be used for multi-purpose leisure activities. Like tennis, for instance. Unfortunately, he hadn't found a way to make the combined radio/photo-album/stethoscope/tennis racket work yet, so that just looked like a conventional tennis racket. All in all, it was a pretty visionary meeting."

Alec: "So, he wasn't just a tennis pro who's secretly seeing your secretary and she's got him drawing a salary as a fake consultant?"

Sir Terrence: "I hardly think they would have been taken in so easily. No, he was the real McCoy. Although, the rumourmongers did suggest he was open to the occasional back-hander. Now I'm doing it! These suggestions are unbelievably infectious. Critics just don't appreciate success, and the public always believe the worst, simply because no field of human endeavour likes it's tall poppies. Then again, nowadays, some of the weeds grow pretty darn high too. I should know. I've promoted some of them.

I don't like to put my own ex-employees down, but they were, shall we say, improvising. The mark boy, who previously operated the flipchart at meetings, just went round cancelling things. He scrapped the business lunches, gym memberships, corporate hospitality boxes, golden hellos, golden farewells, my rescue and the political fund to bribe, er, not bribe – that's such an ugly word. The fund was to 'lobby' politicians and thus guide them into doing the right thing for business. Most of them were open to a little guidance, but it did require quite an extensive consultancy budget. The more 'guided' of them became non-attending directors, which gave us an unexpected saving on biscuits at board meetings.

Then there was that ridiculous interloper who only comes to the fourteenth floor to change the bottles on the water cooler. He spilt a glassful all over a keyboard and turned the screen to gibberish. Since no one was about, he tried to cover it up by replying to a few emails himself. The little twit seems to have consolidated our Egyptian assets into zinc futures and earned a net profit of one hundred and seventy one million pounds. How was a responsible executive meant to explain that at the AGM? They did, of course, extend the lease on the watercoolers for the next financial year. They're on the thirteenth floor now.

The problem of being short staffed soon took on a more sinister aspect. Employees were so rushed that they didn't have time to implement the self assessment exercise, fill out the quarterly appraisal forms, attend the time and motion study, appraise their workspace ergonomy requirements, email jokes to their friends, arrange the motivational de-tox management training weekends with our corporate holistic self-awareness guru, at the usual country hotel, or any of the other essentials. Apparently, the trainer on the training course to train you how to take training courses started to question her purpose in life. Whilst staff were waiting for their instructions, they had to um, they had to actually get on with their jobs instead."

Alec: "We could have finished this tree by now."

Sir Terrence: "The market was soon swamped with rumours and I wasn't there to stop them. Stories about us, stories about our competitors. A ridiculous rumour would send a market plummeting and then, as if on cue, the corporation bought in. Just before the end of the year, a rumour circulated that a toy we made was what all the children wanted for Christmas. You should have seen the scrum! A product would be rumoured unavailable and Allied would be ready to fill the gap. Just look at Salad Cream substitutes. St John's Wort. Drinking mineral water because tap water is suddenly unfit for human consumption. Eating only fatty food for long enough will make you lose weight! It would have been amazing to watch, only I couldn't.

The first I knew about it was when the boat failed to arrive and take me to the negotiations to sell the company. They'd cancelled it because of the popular belief that I'd gone missing. I eventually got off the island by diverting a Philippino cargo crew and paying them, in what I thought were my soon-to-collapse business's worthless junk share certificates, and conned myself passage back to Tilbury docks. A long voyage in filthy conditions, but since the ship was teeming with rats and fat cats, the place did rather remind me of my gentleman's club. It was only when they followed me home to see if I had any more share certificates that I thought to check the paper and see what they were worth.

I nearly had a fit! Those rotten cargo-hounds must have known all along! I can't believe that they managed to con me whilst I was trying to con them. I weep for modern morality."

Alec: "I feel like a squirrel."

Sir Terrence: "Stop thinking about your stomach all the time. Breakfast is for wimps. I remember the catastrophic headlines now. Despite a background of global recession, loss of the entire upper management structure and a sudden market downturn, British Allied's sales had gone through the roof. They'd cornered the world market in at least three commodity sectors. I couldn't think of anything worse."

Alec: "Why? I thought you'd have been pleased."

Sir Terrence: "A month or two before I'd realised that under my textbook system of micromanagement, applying all the mistakes I'd learnt from at the airline, the business was still veering toward the potty quicker than I could comfortably disguise. At that rate, they wouldn't even have the funds available to give me an indecently generous pay-off. I therefore instituted the 'Junior Staff Stakeholder Share Scheme'. It was a revolutionary new way to make the staff feel they were part of a great family, with a common purpose, working towards a mutual goal. The other goal was to get some of their salary ploughed back into the current reserves, to fund my pay-off, in return for a reasonable share allocation. This was all on the grounds that the shares would become worthless about five minutes after the auditors arrived."

Alec: "So now the shares have gone through the roof, and junior staff own the corporation. Do they know?"

Sir Terrence: "Well, I'd planned to cover it up at the AGM, but a rumour went round that all the shareholder invitations had been addressed to people in the same building. I supposed that staring into a sea of happy investors faces, all wearing company identification badges, the subterfuge wouldn't last long. Instead, I confronted my secretary. Not just my secretary, but I see now that she was the local operative of the National Association for the Propagation & Dissemination of Rumours."

Alec: "How do you know that?"

Sir Terrence: "Ha! I monitored some of her little chats. The woman simply thrives on the internet. You can not overestimate the power of this individual. If she takes offence at a kebab shop, one mention of the word 'Alsatian' and the place is closed by nightfall. You want to know who started the whisper that 'brown is the new black'? Guess? If she wants to make sunburn fashionable she'll just suggest in the right places that red is the new brown. Have you ever wondered who nobbled that weather forecaster back in '87 to say the hurricane wasn't coming? She even suggested at the Christmas party that Father Christmas wasn't real. Talk about the worm in the bud feeding on the damask. Cheek! This organisation makes Fu Manchu look torpid. There are thousands of these malevolent, grotty little people in offices all over the world spreading conspiracies about kidnapped aliens and corporations withholding low energy environmentally-friendly power sources."

Alec: "Well, I had heard…"

Sir Terrence: "Okay, so they had to get one right. Law of averages."

Alec: "They don't have any real power though, do they? It's all rubbish floating about in people's heads."

Sir Terrence: "The power of belief is one of the greatest forces affecting humanity. It's always been strongest in aspects like god and country, but that's all starting to fade isn't it? They're sowing the seeds of their own destruction though. The public are a sceptical lot these days. If general belief in the unprovable fades, rumours may also start to lose their power. NAPDR is about to institute a plan to reverse the trend, by presenting us with new gods and new flags to believe in. The strategy is to increase the number of people who believe things on faith alone. For example, less people are going to church nowadays aren't they? Even devout believers are starting to wonder why they really need a certain shaped building, a ceremony handing over money, or a bloke in a dress in order to talk to a deity who's supposed to be everywhere and sees all. It's reached a crisis point. Diluted belief. They've lost the multitude. You mark my words, rumours of the second coming are only just around the corner!"

Alec: "Don't get worked up. You'll fall off your perch."

Sir Terrence: "Oh, right. I see that. Well, the bottom line is that I turned the tables on them. Flipley was too smart for me, but I cornered the other one. As I said, she's a strange, incomprehensible woman from the Balkans. Not the most indispensable of secretaries, and she knows it. It came to a head when I called her in and went straight to the point over the tennis coach fiasco. "Vishmilla, I'm going to have to let you go"."

Alec: "Mamma Mia! What did she say?"

Sir Terrence: " "Do not let me go", of course. I really hadn't expected such a song and dance over it. Then she began the most extraordinary series of threats about destroying my reputation. This was my cue. "Hold that thought", I said, "and now invert it". In essence, I demanded they make up a rumour which would give me a reputation-building, face-saving, and lucrative escape route."

Alec: "Up a tree."

Sir Terrence: "No, don't be ridiculous. Vishmilla and her shadowy cronies drafted a rumour that I'd soon be awarded a knighthood and appointed to the Executive Steering Committee of the Cabal of British Industries to trial a selection of uninhabited islands and report on their potential adaptation for executive use. They wrote a speech for the Annual General Meeting in which I took full credit for the stunningly futuristic strategy of releasing full staff potential through executive removal crisis induction. It was so good, I nearly believed it myself. That was more or less the point where I threw it all away."

Alec: "I can see my house from up here."

Sir Terrence: "It must have been the audience reaction that threw me. It all just went to my head. I've never been cheered by share holders before. After I'd finished congratulating myself on my 'vision' I started to drift off the prepared script. At first it was magnanimous enough. "The credit for our dominant market position and astounding sales figures does not rest entirely with me. No, no, really it doesn't, you're too kind. It was partly due to the climate of fear and threatened job security that my fellow directors engendered when they instinctively followed my lead and went off on long term sick leave claiming executive stress. Yes, I'm proud of my returning management team and would hope they will continue to rubber stamp my enormous and thoroughly deserved self-calculated pay rise, share options and productivity bonuses, as I will reciprocally continue to do for them. A-hem.""

Alec: "They chased you out of the building then?"

Sir Terrence: "Into the Thames. I had no idea I floated so well. Obviously the cream floats to the top."

Alec: "That's not the only thing I've seen floating in the Thames."

Sir Terrence: "You didn't believe what they said about me afterwards did you? You don't think I'm greedy?"

Alec: "Well, you are a fat cat stuck in a tree."

Sir Terrence: "You are coming to work again tomorrow, aren't you?"

Alec: "Oh, look. I think I can see a fire engine."

GAVIN THE BULB

Cast of characters

Tom an airline co-pilot, awaiting his flight
Mr C. Thaw a new arrival in cabin crew uniform
Pilot Hugo Bitpart (no relation)

People bustled, newspapers rustled, in the crew lounge at Hastings International Airport…

Tom: "Hi. I'm the co-pilot for the Potsdam flight. I've not been here before. Is this where we wait?"

Mr C: "Yes, that's right. I'm just waiting for my flight too. Time for a chat? You can plonk down next to me if you like. I'm cabin crew myself. I've been at this lark for a while, but the hanging about still gets to me."

Tom: "Have you had a go on the new airport simulator? No? All the very latest in interactive entertainment. It simulates the whole experience of being in an airport. Waiting mostly. That, overpriced coffee and the occasional plasticised snack. To be honest it's not worth the five quid, but it gives the kids something to do. Are you okay?"

Mr C: "Strange really, but I still get nervous before a job. All this waiting gets me expectant, if you know what I mean. I spend a lot of time in airports. Now, of course, it's the safest form of travel."

Tom: "Most people forget that don't they? In training they tell you to focus on the routine. Nowadays, for the pilot, it's mostly just take-off and landing. The rest is all down to trusting the automation. There doesn't really need to be a pilot at all, but the public wouldn't have the confidence to fly without one. I'm the co-pilot, so I've trained for years and I've got even less to do. Still, shouldn't complain. It's a more interesting career than most."

Mr C: "It's a chaotic world though. Anything can go wrong. The passengers want someone there for the day when something happens which the programmers don't know about. That's where you come in. A butterfly flaps it's wings and the leaning tower of Pisa changes colour, that sort of thing."

Tom: "Yes, I suppose you're right. Although you can see why the designers want to ease human error out of the equation, seeing as people are the cause of most accidents."

Mr C: "That reminds me of a funny story. There was a bloke who hitched a lift on an oil tanker. You can do that you know. Commercial shipping always has a berth or two for paying passengers. He wandered up to the bridge some nights and had chats with the Captain. They'd play cards and he'd drink rum while the Captain had his orange-juice. He'd notice how the Captain had a lot of time on his hands unless a beeper or flashing light went off to let him know something was happening. Even then it was difficult to do much about it as the ship took around four miles to slow down. It was a hulking great thing too, the Flexon Mynese they called it.

Anyway, one evening they were approaching Newfoundland when he dropped a real clanger. "It takes the skill out of captaincy now it's all run by computer. You're job's just turned into babysitting in a smart uniform". With that, the Captain reached for the bottle of rum to chase him off the bridge, but then thought to himself that wasn't appropriate behaviour for a captain and poured himself a drink from it instead. "You're talking rubbish! We're all very highly trained." They chatted about the march of technology and suchlike, then poured themselves another drink to sharpen their debating skills. "So" says your man, "you could get this thing into port if all the computers crashed?" The Captain nodded vociferously. "I could steer this crate by feel alone! Every shudder of the engine is like a familiar thingee. It's an old friend, this ship. We've been across the world and back. Back the other way of course. Have another drink." The Captain must have thought that was an end to it."

He carried on though, which is something you really shouldn't do to people with important jobs. "It's easy though isn't it? Not a lot of traffic about either. I could get this thing into harbour; you just have to aim it roughly in the right direction and if you're a bit off, you've got hours to nudge it back onto the right path." The Captain nearly exploded. "Where did you get that from? It takes years to understand a system like this!" "Face facts, it's not a skilled job nowadays. Intuition and the old sea-dog spirit simply isn't going to make a difference anymore." They refilled their glasses.

"There's much more to it than that", he said. "You've got to have a working knowledge of the waters, the tides and currents. The ship sounds different when it hits a new cross stream. You've got to carry a map in your head like the back of your hand". "Have another drink, oh, the rum's all gone. Never mind. Where was I? You'll have to face it mate, it's not a skilled job anymore and the ship's automatic, so there's no way you can even prove it." The Captain snorted in defiance "Ruddy is! I could get this thing home with all the computers switched off, blindfold, just by the vibrations the propellers make!" "I bet you couldn't" "Ruddy can!" "Right, money where your mouth is! Five dollars!" "You're on". Of course, after the Captain removed the blindfold, his passenger was gone. He made five dollars though. They spent years clearing up the oil."

Tom: "That's dreadful. One person caused all that damage with just a friendly chat? There should be a law."

Mr C: "I agree. The man, the passenger in the story, had a history of changing things just by talking to people. It's not just automation you see, it's the butterfly wing situation happening again. He lent someone a bottletop during the Pakistan Test Series of '94. Reverse swing they called it. Made the papers. Then there was that stocks and shares thing in '87 when he said "You want to affect the markets? I know a good joke: How about if we all decided to sell at once!"

Of course, I put most of that down to his great-grandfather's influence. He was the shovel salesman who arrived in California before the Goldrush, built a shovel shop, stocked up with thirty thousand shovels and people said he'd gone mad. Then, one dark night, he crept out to the little stream running out of the mountains and planted one, very yellow, nugget of gold. Do you want to know why there are no passenger pigeons? It's because he met an obsessive gun-nut on his way home from the bar, pointed out a flock of pigeons and said "They're talking about you, you know." That's not the best effort I heard of. His grandfather did a doozy, although he never liked to talk about it. Of course, it was talking about it that got all the trouble started in the first place."

Tom: "What do you mean? What trouble?"

Mr C: "Well, he was up in the hills of Bosnia talking to this Austrian guardsman who was getting bored with guarding some raggedy flag as it was such a hot day. The birds were singing too, which doesn't help. Grandfather gave him a drink and they got talking. "The rifle they've palmed you off with has seen better days" and the soldier replies "This is a precision instrument! The best Austro-Hungary has to offer!" So he says "Rubbish. I know sub-standard kit when I see it. What's the range on that thing?" The guard thinks about this and announces he can hit a shed on the next ridge. Grandfather gives him another drink and mentions all foreigners being poor shots. The guard shoots the shed and has a drink of slivovitz to celebrate winning the argument.

It's strong stuff, that plum brandy, so grandfather continues. "Alright, so you can hit the back end of a barn despite the equipment being rubbish. Call that a challenge? What can you see in the valley down there? That's what I'd call shooting" "Well, there's the procession and the fellow in the ridiculous uniform at the front." "Don't be daft," says grandpa "That's twice as far as I meant." The soldier has a flash of national pride "Not far enough for me". "'Course, that's well out of range, but there it is". The guard looks indignant. "Oh, no it isn't!" "Right! Money where your mouth is. Five dinars!" He got to his feet. "Right, you're on!" When the guard turned around a few minutes later, there was no grandpa, just a few coins on the grass where he'd been sitting. There was a hell of a fuss about Arch-Duke Franz Ferdinand, but five dinars was a fortune to a young lad in 1914."

Tom: "Blimey! It has to be co-incidence though. Affecting chaos? You'd never get a feel for something that complicated. Forget automation, it would be like having the key to the Universe. Are you saying that all these disasters happened just because of talking to people?"

Mr C: "Not just disasters, no. In my experience chaos is a fairly neutral force. It's much the same with automation. Sometimes it turns out quite well."

Tom: "What does the initial 'C' on your name badge stand for?"

Mr C: "Chas. That's why I gave up the idea of training to be a pilot really. The airline said they can't have pilots called 'Chas'. The travelling public wouldn't have confidence. Would I like to do airfreight? I don't see what difference a name makes. I've got a cousin Lilith back in London who's very high up in the railways. Responsible job. Making sure trains meet their connections, postal freight doesn't get lost, that sort of thing. She's always good for a natter."

Tom: "I've got a sister called Anne. She works in a library. She's a librarian. Sorry, mind wandering. I was just thinking how your name just needs an 'o' to spell 'chaos'."

Mr C: "Doesn't matter. Nothing really does in the long run. Did anyone ever tell you the story of Gavin and the lighthouse?"

Tom: "No. What was that? You'd better tell me quickly because I'm meant to be in the cockpit."

Mr C: "I only need another minute."

Tom: "Alright then. Tell me the story."

Mr C: "He came on a visit. A cultural exchange I think, with a lad from Doncaster. The other children thought he was a bit dim, but no one said anything. As the year went by, he got progressively brighter. It even affected the school league tables. When his time was nearly up, they gave him a scholarship to carry on. He worked with some brilliant people at university, but he always overshadowed them. He had to leave in the end because he woke up one day and he'd gone luminescent."

Tom: "Luminescent?"

Mr C: "Yes, that's right. 20,000 candlepower. It hurt just to look at him. There was only one thing for it. He decided to go somewhere where he could remain inconspicuous."

Tom: "How on Earth did he manage that?"

Mr C: "One day, when there was nobody around because there was something good on the telly, Gavin slipped away and got a job as a lighthouse-keeper. There were lots of jobs as lighthouse keepers because people aren't queuing up to live in a cold tower, in the middle of nowhere, all on their own for years and years. He didn't even need an interview. After all, they thought, how many Gavins could it possibly take to change a light bulb? Forget training. Well then, he lived in a lighthouse, where the black rocks guard against the sea."

Tom: "Isn't that Noggin the Nog?"

Mr C: "Oh, sorry, I was going into storytelling mode. Force of habit. For the first few years, Gavin liked living in the lighthouse. There was plenty of room and a great view of the ocean. He could glow as much as he wanted at night and there weren't nosy people about to ask what was going on. Even the seagulls got used to it after a while, although the new ones kept blinking a lot and bumping into things. Gavin soon became the best seagull-doctor there ever was and then got to the root of the problem by making them all little pairs of tinted flying-goggles which they sometimes used for snorkelling. That could explain why snorkels have become such an endangered species in coastal waters.

It wasn't an ideal life though. Gavin ran such a successful lighthouse that no shipwrecked mariners ever knocked on his door wanting rescuing and a mug of tea. That was a shame because he made good tea. There wasn't much to do at all, apart from taking messages by Morse code. Most of them weren't for him, but he wrote them down anyway to keep up with what everyone else was doing. Hey up, he thought, I'll try fishing! The fish always saw him coming, so there wasn't much point in that, but he did it anyway. Dangling, he called it. Still, it was good to dip his incandescent toes into something, even if it was a bay full of absolutely no fish. He never found out of course, but when his toes were in the water, no fish were ever known to crash into the rocks.

Gavin had lots of time to himself in the lighthouse, so practised balancing things on his nose and shadow puppetry. Sometimes he did both things at once, which was amazing, had there been anyone there to amaze. In fact, after several years, he became able to balance anything in the lighthouse on the end of his nose. Starting with spoons and things, he worked his way up to wheelbarrows and the big rack to put the lifejackets on. Bottles were his favourites though. They reflected the light all round the room and mesmerised the seagull community. Towards the end he could balance a seagull on the kitchen sink, with all the washing up, on a wheelbarrow, on the thing with the lifejackets, on a bottle, on the end of his nose. Then he had to have a bit of a rest before a long stint of sitting up all night shimmering."

Tom: "Sounds idyllic."

Mr C: "I suppose it was. At least, it was until things started going wrong. Progress they called it. He wrote down the Morse code one day and was surprised to discover the message was addressed to him. He had to double check because there'd never been a letter for him before. The message said that the lighthouse was going to be automated so that no one would have to waste their time living in it anymore. It said 'thank you for your sterling service all these years in the saving of so many sailor-related lives', and 'you're fired' so 'hop it'. They'd even mentioned a date when he had to be out by. They were

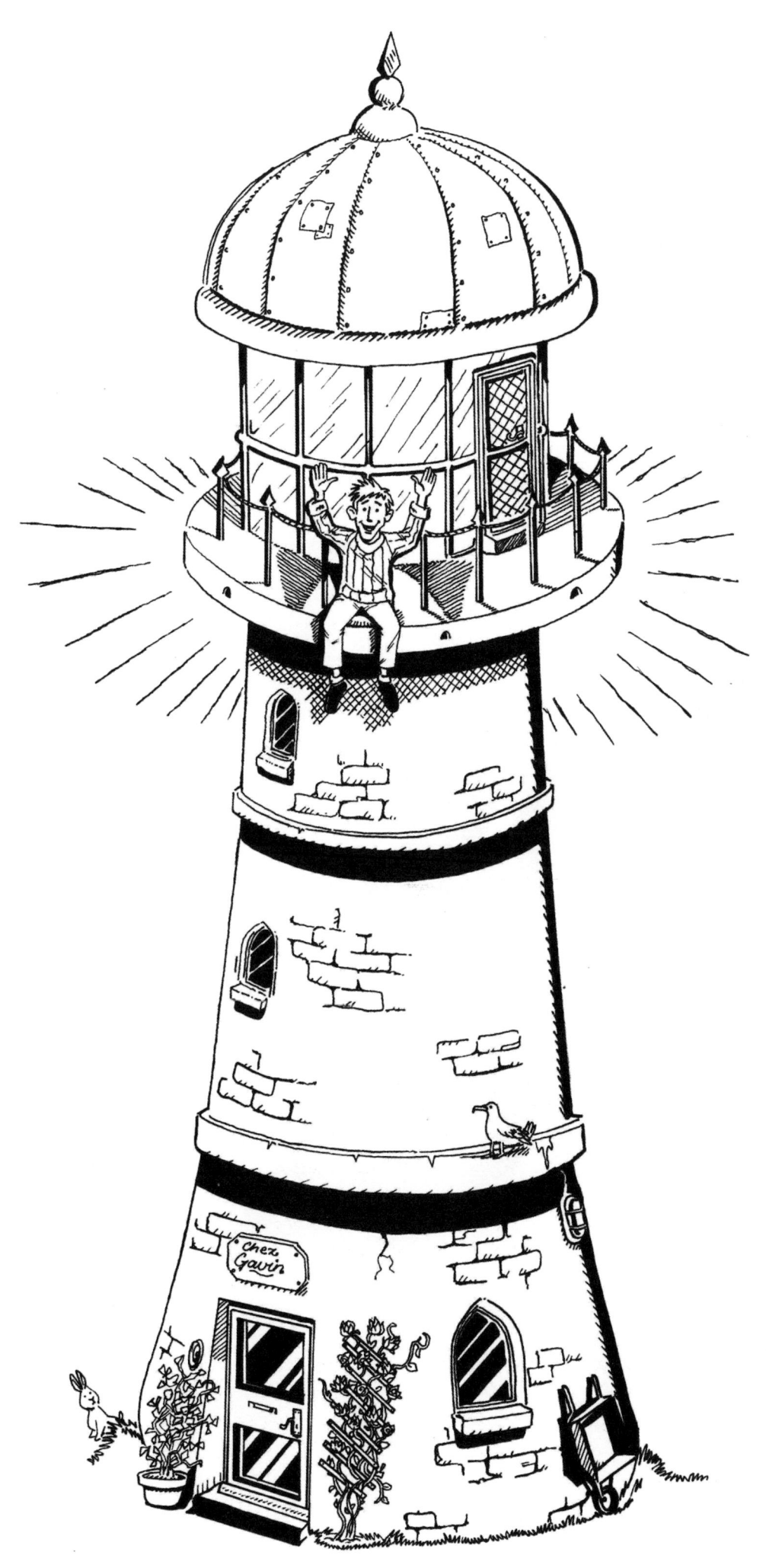

thoughtful like that. Gavin didn't want to leave. Gavin couldn't leave. He stayed in the lighthouse doing the only thing he knew how, apart from the balancing and shadow puppetry, until the day for leaving had come and gone. How could he live a normal life outside the lighthouse? People would think he was a freak and do experiments on him. How would he ever be accepted among normal people? He spent an hour or two wondering what a normal person was. Hmmm, difficult.

Gavin wrote to all the normal people he could think of in the outside world, from all his code messages and the long wave radio. He wrote to the Queen, the Emperor of Japan, the man who interrupts the cricket with the shipping forecast (he *must* be important to get away with that) and Jumbo Ragga The Skiffle Man. The Queen was busy with the horses, so someone wrote back for her asking Gavin to stop 'pulling her leg'. Gavin didn't understand that bit and supposed they'd got him mixed up with someone else. He wouldn't have the temerity to pull the Queen.

Some of the others at least tried to give him some support. The Emperor of Japan sent a ninja with all the powers of the Nine-Han Kati! He wasn't much help. He just sulked a lot and complained the noodles were off. That was as nothing to what he said when Gavin put milk in his tea. He had to go in the end when he broke the lifebelt post. Not only was that vandalising property, but there's clearly a limit to that sort of behaviour in a built up area. Gavin pointed out that there was nothing so built up as a lighthouse and locked him out. The ninja agreed, apologised, and melted away into the shadows, which weren't there fifteen seconds before and had gone by the time Gavin came out to check.

The shipping report person said there wasn't much he could do, since his job was just to spoil the cricket when it got to the good bit with lots of made-up stuff about Finisterre and Cromarty, but he'd mention it to his friends who do the gardening show on Tuesdays. Jumbo Ragga

The Skiffle Man wrote him a very kind letter, with colourful stamps from Jamaica, and said to 'be cool'. Then, on his birthday, the lights went out. Or rather, they didn't. The lighthouse owners had shut off the electricity and stood on the cliffs waiting for the great beam of light to fade and die. Strangely, it didn't. Curiously, sometimes it went downstairs a flight or two and got itself a cup of tea. 'Batteries', they thought, so tried to raise Gavin on the radio. The radio wasn't working.

'Something strange going on here' said the foreman and waved away at a seagull in dark glasses. The seagull waved back. The waves just sat there. It was then that Gavin decided to take Mr Jumbo's advice and step outside to find out what the world had planned for him next. Gavin resolved, there and then, to be cool. The line of frozen wide-eyed rabbits on the headland was, frankly, nothing to do with him. He thought that perhaps he could put the shining beacon thing down to an industrial injury."

Tom: "How did he manage?"

Mr C: "They called him 'Gavin The Bulb' at first. Of course, nobody ever told him that he was the re-incarnation of Pitcherpikapotchakettle, the Mayan sun-god. I think it's because they mainly make chocolate in the region now, so the last thing they need is him coming back and melting it. The descendents of the Mayans thought England was a much better place for him, all in all. "They've got a better way of dealing with inexplicable cultural differences", said the South American shaman to the helpful lady from the student exchange programme. "South Americans fall to their knees and worship people like Gavin."

"In England", the shaman explained, "if folk see anything unusual, they get very polite and persuade themselves it's not actually happening." As it turned out, that was more or less exactly what they did.

In Gavin's new village there were no huts, no rainforest clearings and they only made burnt offerings on the fast food stand at the annual fete. The villagers were different too. They'd pointedly ignore the fact he's a sun-god and marvel at the whole bottle-balancing exhibition. After a while they just referred to him as 'whatsit – the fellow with the… I wonder if it hurts his nose?', then 'the bottle-balancing chappie' and one day it became 'Gav', then eventually 'Our Gav'.

Gavin got invited to the pub a lot more nowadays, even when there wasn't a powercut. His friends drank bitter, but he stuck to light. Especially in the winter, people liked socialising when Gavin was around. After a while he thought he was a pool-god, but he knew he wasn't really. They stopped him playing when the green baize curled up at the corners. Sometimes he'd help the landlord fetch the barrels up from the dark, damp cellar. He'd never seen a dark cellar, and it didn't stay damp for long either.

The landlord spoke to the brewery and turned the cellar into a solarium. They put Gavin in charge, where he stayed happy for the rest of his days with lots of friends, a few steps from the pub and with no ships to worry about ever, ever again. Only the seagulls missed him. Sometimes, just sometimes, he'd get a letter from a lad from Doncaster who's loving his life as a

Mayan witch-doctor."

Pilot Bitpart [arriving and sounding exasperated]: "Hey! Where have you been? Chatting? Our flight's late for take off now. I'll have to report this to the Civil Aviation Authority you know. You're for the high-jump!"

Tom: "I don't know how it happened. I'm sorry, I was miles away. Anyway, what difference is a minute going to make?"

There is a huge tearing, rumbling, jet aircraft noise…

Pilot [shocked]: "Hey! Did you see that? A plane's just slewed straight across our runway! I call that a bit of a lucky escape."

The co-pilot turned on his heel, very slowly, to the suddenly empty row of seats behind him…

Tom: Hello? I say! Hello?…